PRAISE FOR *SAYING YES*

As I meet and challenge people to discover and respond to God's will on their life's journey, I always wonder what resource I can offer them. *Saying Yes* "scratches where we itch." Albert Haase, OFM, has provided a blueprint and road map for discovering all the places, all the spaces, and all the faces through which God speaks to us. *Saying Yes* is down-to-earth spirituality at its best!

—MOST REVEREND FERNAND J. CHERI, III, OFM,
Auxiliary Bishop of New Orleans

∎

Saying Yes is a practical handbook for discerning the ways in which God speaks to us in and through our daily experiences. Albert Haase, OFM, reminds us that each of us is called to speak an ever-deepening yes to God with our lives. The text centers around the most basic questions of the spiritual life: What are we living for? What keeps us from being fully alive? It brings the deep sources of the Christian tradition alive with stories, helpful quotations, and probing questions. Haase offers a faithful and faith-filled reflection on both the simplicity and the complexity of Christian discernment and discipleship.

—MOST REVEREND DONALD BOLEN, Bishop of Saskatoon

∎

Saying Yes—the title alone conveys what a positive, life-giving, soul-feeding approach to discernment this book is. Albert Haase's advice herein for coming to know the will of God for our lives is both invitational and life-changing. Read this important book—you will be encouraged and better for it!

—J. BRENT BILL, author of *Life Lessons from a Bad Quaker*

∎

Albert Haase sets out the Christian practice of discernment as a way of continually saying "yes" to God's dreams for each of us, our communities, and the world.

—ELIZABETH LIEBERT, SNJM, Professor of Spiritual Life
and Director of the Program in Christian Spirituality
at San Francisco Theological Seminary

ALBERT HAASE, OFM

SAYING
yes

DISCOVERING AND RESPONDING
TO GOD'S WILL IN YOUR LIFE

PARACLETE PRESS
BREWSTER, MASSACHUSETTS

2016 First printing

Saying Yes: Discovering and Responding to God's Will in Your Life

Copyright © 2016 by Franciscan Friars of the State of Missouri

ISBN 978-1-61261-761-9

Library of Congress Cataloging-in-Publication Data

Names: Haase, Albert, 1955-
Title: Saying yes : discovering and responding to God's will in your life /
   Albert Haase, OFM.
Description: Brewster MA : Paraclete Press Inc., 2015. | Includes
   bibliographical references.
Identifiers: LCCN 2015033524 | ISBN 9781612617619
Subjects: LCSH: Discernment (Christian theology) | Listening—Religious
   aspects—Christianity.
Classification: LCC BV4509.5 .H23 2015 | DDC 248.4--dc23
LC record available at http://lccn.loc.gov/2015033524

10 9 8 7 6 5 4 3 2 1

Published by Paraclete Press
Brewster, Massachusetts
www.paracletepress.com

Printed in the United States of America

Though I have no fear of God and no respect for anyone,
yet because this widow keeps bothering me, I will grant her justice, so
that she may not wear me out by continually coming.

—*Luke 18:4–5*

CONTENTS

O ne of the most challenging spiritual practices for any committed Christian is discerning the will of God. What is God asking of me? How do I know if this is really of God and not simply my imagination? Where do I turn to find out what God wants? Should I follow my head or my heart? Do my deep-seated, recurring desires confirm or conflict with God's will? We all have asked these or similar questions at some point in time.

As a spiritual director and as someone who trains spiritual directors, I have spent a lot of time listening to the discernment struggles of others and reflecting on what the spiritual tradition has taught about discernment. I'm not the only one. Do a quick search on Amazon.com, and you'll discover enough books on discerning God's will to fill a library.

So why another book on discernment? Because *Saying Yes: Discovering and Responding to God's Will in Your Life* highlights in a singular way that authentic Christian discernment requires daily listening to the megaphone God uses to communicate with us: the nitty-gritty of everyday life. Like the persistent widow in Luke's parable (see Lk. 18:1–8), God invites each of us to respond uniquely to the dream of the kingdom. And then God waits. When our response is not forthcoming, God returns and invites again. And again, if necessary. No wonder so much of discernment is listening and reflecting on our life; without that deepening self-knowledge and continual self-awareness, we could spend our lives dawdling and lollygagging.

Why this book? Because *Saying Yes: Discovering and Responding to God's Will in Your Life* shows how an adversary is bent on sabotaging our response to God's long-term plan for our glorious living. I have yet to find a book on discernment that clearly unmasks the devious designs of the devil and how the powers of darkness conspire against our response to the divine widow.

Why this book? Because *Saying Yes: Discovering and Responding to God's Will in Your Life* directly addresses a topic discussed in spiritual direction sessions but rarely written about: how we often wrestle with God and resist divine grace. Discernment includes not only discovering when God is calling us but also when, how, and why we fight against God's invitation.

In these pages, you will meet various people whom I have known or have been privileged to sit with in spiritual direction sessions. I've changed their names and some personal details to protect their privacy.

This little book will show how discernment is not confined to moments when we stand before two divergent roads and must choose a direction for our continued journey. Discernment is a daily spiritual practice of discovering in big and small ways the invitation of God to say yes to becoming a coworker for the kingdom.

Albert Haase, OFM

CHAPTER 1

GOD'S DREAM OF THE KINGDOM

∎

For the first thirty years of my life, I understood God's will as a master blueprint or detailed script that had already been predetermined and written. As I figured, on the day of my conception, God had decided the role I was going to play in the history of salvation. I assumed I was supposed to spend the early part of my life "picking God's brain" to see what God demands of me. Once I discovered my preassigned vocation, I had to buckle under and fulfill it. I hoped I had discerned correctly what God intended for me—to be a Franciscan friar and a priest—though I wouldn't know if I got it right until the day I die.

I imagined that after my death I would stand outside the Pearly Gates. St. Peter would come out and ask my name. "Albert Haase," I would reply. He would go to the filing cabinet, open the drawer marked "H," and find the folder containing my permanent record. St. Peter would then pass it on to God, who sat on the throne of judgment.

Flipping through my folder, God would ask, "Well, Albert Haase, what have you done for yourself?" I would reply very confidently, "Lord, I became a Franciscan friar and was ordained a priest." I would keep my fingers crossed that God wouldn't grimace, shake his head, and say, "Sorry, buddy. You got it all wrong! You were supposed to be married with three children and teach in a high school!" If God did, I would discover only then and there that my entire life had been wasted.

Pagan Fate or a Godly Dream?

I became uncomfortable with this understanding of God's will. Though it sounds wonderful to say that God called me to be a Franciscan priest from the moment of my existence, or that God intended you to marry your spouse from the moment you entered the world, there's a problem with such thinking: it smacks of the pagan notion of fate. It makes everything in this world a predetermined and preordained done deal; my eternal reward and happiness are not based upon my freely chosen, creative response to the grace of God in my life—what I call my yes—but rather on whether I managed to guess and find my preassigned role in God's plan of salvation history and then performed it.

Is there really such a thing as God's will? If so, how are we to understand it without falling into the trap of fate or predestination? Let me quote from the first chapter of the letter to the Ephesians. Here's the paraphrase from THE MESSAGE:

> How blessed is God! And what a blessing he is! He's the Father
> of our Master, Jesus Christ, and takes us to the high places of
> blessing in him. Long before he laid down earth's foundations,
> he had us in mind, had settled on us as the focus of his love,
> to be made whole and holy by his love. Long, long ago he

decided to adopt us into his family through Jesus Christ. (What pleasure he took in planning this!) He wanted us to enter into the celebration of his lavish gift-giving by the hand of his beloved Son. . . .

He thought of everything, provided for everything we could possibly need, letting us in on the plans he took such delight in making. He set it all out before us in Christ, a long-range plan in which everything would be brought together and summed up in him, everything in deepest heaven, everything on planet earth.

It's in Christ that we find out who we are and what we are living for. Long before we first heard of Christ and got our hopes up, he had his eye on us, had designs on us for glorious living, part of the overall purpose he is working out in everything and everyone. (Eph.1:3–6, 8–12, 14)

Rather than "God's will," I prefer the phrase "God's dream." At the dawn of creation, God had a dynamic, evolving dream for us—a "long-range plan," to use the words from THE MESSAGE paraphrase. Even before the creation of the world, God had us in mind and with voracious enthusiasm wanted us to be the focus of a transformative love that would make us whole and holy. God's openhanded and extravagant generosity would be centered upon us. And God delighted in planning this! God would adopt us into a divine family through his Son Jesus, who reveals to us our identity and mission. In the fullness of time as this world evolves and becomes more complex and intricate, God's dynamic dream is that we take our place with all creation under the lordship of Jesus Christ.

Original Sin

That dream was quickly tarnished. With Adam and Eve's freely chosen sin of wanting to be like God and thus eating the forbidden fruit, all of creation got knocked out of whack. That original sin had a ripple effect, first seen in the murder of Abel by Cain, that continues to affect us today. Just look at the world, and you will see war, violence, hatred, prejudice, and injustice. World peace, unconditional love, and justice for all seem so distant and unattainable. Indeed, creation has a long way to go before it comes under the lordship of Jesus Christ.

But Adam and Eve's sin could neither dampen God's voracious enthusiasm for us nor cancel God's designs on us for glorious living. God's dream was indomitable. As human history unfolded and evolved, God deliberately entered into intentional relationships, called covenants, with Abraham, Isaac, and Jacob. These patriarchs represented the chosen people, God's "cherished, personal treasure" (Deut. 7:6, THE MESSAGE). God desired both the patriarchs and the chosen people to be dream keepers who kept God's dream alive by living lives of peace, love, and justice. By exercising their free will, they would be coworkers with God in making the dream come true.

Prophetic Reminders

The chosen people, heirs of Adam and Eve's sin, weren't always faithful to God's covenant. So God raised up prophets who reminded the chosen people that the world was not as God intended and chastised the people's misguided, egotistical, sinful behavior. The prophets called the people to return to the covenant with God and keep the dream alive: to cease doing evil, learning to do good, seeking justice, rescuing the oppressed, defending the orphan, and pleading for the widow (see Isa. 1:17). Only then could the dream once again gain a foothold in reality.

. . . [O]nly after the "fiat" of Mary, who consented to be the Mother of the Messiah, did "the angel depart from her" (Lk. 1:38). The angel had completed his mission: he could bring to God humanity's "yes", spoken by Mary of Nazareth.

—Pope St. John Paul II[1]

At the beginning of the first century, women were considered second-class citizens. Their sworn testimony was inadmissible in court; they were considered the property of their spouses with no legal claim to property of their own. So the only "property" a woman could call her own was her reputation. At a precise moment in history, God entered the life of one member of the chosen people, a woman by the name of Mary, and asked her to sacrifice that one thing—her reputation—and become the mother of Jesus. Surprisingly and at the initial consternation of her fiancé,

Mary said yes to God and became Theotokos, the "God-bearer," the first and greatest title she continues to bear as a member of the human race.

God's voracious enthusiasm and lavish gift-giving erupts in the person of Mary's son, Jesus. Jesus is the divine reminder of the dream. He called it "the kingdom." In more than twenty Gospel stories and parables, he reminded his followers that the kingdom is a place of peace, love, and justice. And he didn't just preach the kingdom; Jesus orchestrated the reality of the kingdom in deed. In his life, death, and resurrection—what we call the Paschal Mystery—creation, knocked out of whack by Adam and Eve's sin, got back on track. The kingdom was manifest, and, to this very day, we are on the way to experiencing the fulfillment of God's long-range plan.

Coworkers with Christ

In April 1955, I came into the world. As a human being, I continue to experience the ripple effects of Adam and Eve's egotistical ploy to be like God. And so I find myself tempted and sometimes wrapped up in what St. Paul calls the "works of the flesh": fornication, impurity, licentiousness, idolatry, sorcery, enmities, strife, jealousy, anger, quarrels, dissensions, factions, envy, drunkenness, and carousing (see Gal. 5:19–21). I choose to be deceptive, divisive, and discouraging.

And yet my baptism and commitment to Christ witness to who I am and what I am living for, to allude again to the paraphrase of Ephesians. I am God's dream keeper, and my mission is to make God's dream present in my own life by living a life of peace, love, and justice. Following the example of Mary, I affirm and reaffirm—I say yes—to being a coworker in building the kingdom of God and promoting the lordship of Jesus Christ over all creation.

Grace and Discernment

My chosen identity in Christ and its subsequent mission are not assumed and realized by sheer willpower. Nor do they exclusively rely upon a single life decision or my limited perception. God's voracious enthusiasm for my glorious living is experienced as grace that emboldens and illumines my commitment—and sometimes, as it did in Mary's life, invites me to respond creatively to a specific circumstance or situation. *Discernment is a cooperative venture of discovering my unique contribution—my evolving and deeper yes—to being a coworker with Christ in making God's dream of the kingdom a reality right here, right now.* I call it "my evolving and deeper yes." Why? Because as my circumstances change and I grow in the understanding of who I am and what it means to be a Christian disciple, my perceived contribution as a coworker with Christ will also change and evolve.

What you are is God's gift to you, what you become is your gift to God.

—Hans Urs von Balthasar[2]

In other words, I have God-given talents and abilities. As I grow through childhood, adolescence, and into adulthood, I gradually come to a deeper awareness of who I am as a person. I also learn what it means to be a Christian and how I might use my gifts and skills.

That growing awareness of my identity, including my commitment as a Christian, is ongoing. The vocational choices and daily decisions I make, based upon my identity, interests, and talents, become my contribution to the realization of God's long-range plan, the dream of the kingdom.

An experience from my past offers an apt analogy. I arrived for my first visit to the Grand Canyon rather late in the evening. It was already dark. But my curiosity and excitement at seeing the natural wonder would not wait until morning. So I went to the southern rim to take a look. All I saw through the darkness was a big hole. No splendor, no majesty. I couldn't help but think that this was another one of America's great tourist traps. I went back to my tent, determined that my disappointment was not going to ruin this vacation, and fell asleep.

The following morning I got up before dawn. For years I had heard about the miracle of sunrise over the Grand Canyon. So I started back to the rim, careful not to let any anticipation, of excitement or disappointment, get the better of me. As the morning sun inched its way into the sky and offered light to the earth, the "big hole" suddenly started coming alive with shades of red, purple, blue, and yellow. With hundreds of other people, I found myself "oohing" and "aahing" over God's daily miracle in northern Arizona. It was the same ancient canyon as the night before but, in the light of the morning sun, everything looked so different.

Likewise, the more I consciously allow my commitment to being a dream keeper and coworker with Christ to challenge me, the more clearly I will see the part I can play in salvation history. It will be the same old me, but, seen in the light of my Christian commitment, it will seem so different. My actions and attitudes will take on a deeper meaning. Some of my commitments and obligations might have to change, not because of infidelity, but because of the deepening appreciation for my Christian discipleship and my maturing responsibility and free response to the dream of the kingdom. So discernment is not a question of "picking God's brain" to see what God demands of me. Rather, it's my free, creative response to God's long-range plan in light of my baptismal commitment to being a disciple of Jesus.

All of us can attain to Christian virtue and holiness, no matter in what condition of life we live and no matter what our life work may be.

—St. Francis de Sales[3]

A practical consequence of this understanding of God's dream is that I don't have to do specifically "religious" or "holy" endeavors to be a coworker with Christ. The kingdom needs shoe salesmen, authors, teachers, garbage collectors, parents, computer technicians, bartenders, web designers, hair stylists, and every other kind of occupation. Any vocation or job, performed from a faith perspective, can promote the lordship of Jesus Christ.

I spent a little more than a decade as a missionary in mainland China.

According to the laws of the People's Republic of China, foreign missionaries are forbidden to minister in traditional ways. I spent three years as a university English teacher and then became the director of human resources for an international accounting firm. I was always surprised when family, friends, and friars would e-mail me and say how sorry they were that I couldn't be a "real" missionary who was baptizing babies and spreading the Catholic faith. I had a different perspective: I certainly felt like a "real" missionary, though a newfangled one, as I kept the dream alive and tried to make it become reality as a teacher in the classroom and the boss of the HR department. The patience I exhibited with the struggling student, the fair and dignified treatment of an employee I had to let go, and my determination to rise above the gossip of the English department and the politics of the office were my ways of contributing to God's long-range plan.

Lamps of Revelation

There are six lamps that teach us about God's dream. They illumine and enlighten us about God, God's voracious enthusiasm for us, and the role we each can play in God's long-range plan of the kingdom. They also show us how to get back on track when we find ourselves gravitating toward Paul's "works of the flesh" or committing sin.

The first is the Word of God, *Sacred Scripture*. The *Catechism of the Catholic Church* calls Scripture "the speech of God as it is put down in writing under the breath of the Holy Spirit" (*CCC*, 81). Scripture tells us about God's voracious enthusiasm and deliberate choice to be in a

I give you thanks, O Lord, for having made shine forth this light from the sacred deposit of your Holy Scriptures. As you show me the way I should follow, and give me the desire to follow it, you will also give me the powerful help of your grace so I may tread it with a firm step, and with perseverance.

—St. Eugene de Mazenod[4]

relationship with us. It reveals the Ten Commandments that form the basic contours of our yes to God's voracious enthusiasm and focus us on right relationships with God, others, and self. The words of the prophets keep our feet to the fire as we commit to being coworkers with God. The New Testament letters offer practical advice and encouragement to communities wanting to promote God's long-range plan.

The second lamp that illumines God's dream for us is the Word of God made flesh, *Jesus Christ*. As the paraphrase of Ephesians says, it's in Christ that we discover who we are and what we are living for. In him we see the living and divine embodiment of love, peace, and justice. His teachings on loving God, loving neighbor, forgiving our enemies, and surrendering to the cross are important signposts that keep us on the straight and narrow leading to the full realization of God's dream. His Beatitudes and the Sermon on the

Mount show us the practical and radical implications of saying an even deeper yes to the Ten Commandments. As a committed Christian—which literally means "little Christ"—we say yes to following the teachings of Jesus and imitating him in his life and death.

Some might think that divine revelation—God speaking to us—has stopped with the Word of God written in Scripture and made flesh in Jesus. But God continues to speak! We call God's continuing and ongoing revelation *Sacred Tradition.* Sacred Tradition, for lack of a better analogy, is the light of the Holy Spirit under which we continue to read and reflect upon the Word of God. It offers us insight and wisdom to interpret Scripture and the teachings of Jesus for our contemporary day and age. For example, Sacred Tradition has revealed to us that slavery is not part of God's dream and women and children are not second-class citizens. For Roman Catholics, it provided us with the doctrine of the Immaculate Conception and the dogma of the Assumption of the Blessed Virgin Mary. It also has provided our great social teachings, promoting justice and peace in the world. God continues to reveal aspects of the dream through our reading of the signs of the times under the Spirit's light.

The fourth lamp of revelation is the community of believers called the *Church.* This is the dynamic community that has been entrusted with Jesus's mission of witnessing to and living love, peace, and justice. Over the centuries, the Church has been graced with a corporate wisdom that helps us discover and evaluate the authenticity or inauthenticity of a person's evolving and deeper yes. The Church's incredible support and sage advice reminds us that we help build the kingdom as a family, not as lone rangers.

The Church's *sacraments* are another lamp of revelation. These ritual actions of pouring water, anointing with oil, breaking bread, and celebrating God's forgiveness and healing and God's abiding presence in love relationships help us not only grow in the life of the spirit but also give us the wisdom, strength, and fortitude to be faithful coworkers with Christ. The sacraments are encounters with God that reenergize the community of believers in their mission.

The final lamp of revelation is *personal prayer*. In personal dialogue with God at home and during communal worship services at church, I gain deeper insights into my Christian identity as well as my unique and singular contribution to salvation history. Moments of prayer provide the interior space and sacred silence where God speaks words of invitation. In many ways, the first five lamps of revelation provide the oil for this sixth and final lamp.

Kathy's Experience

A number of years ago, I had a spiritual directee, Kathy, whose experience shows how a person's yes evolves and deepens as it is illumined by the lamps of revelation. A practicing Catholic all her life, Kathy studied law at the University of Chicago and, after graduation, accepted a job at a prestigious firm. Within five years she had gained both the respect of her colleagues and a reputation as a fine lawyer. During those years, however, she also began to see and experience the harsh injustices of the American legal system. "Basically, Father, only the rich can afford to have justice served," she told me during a spiritual direction session.

After months of soul searching, which included a weekend retreat, daily prayer, steeping herself in Scripture, and attending Sunday Eucharist, Kathy realized she risked losing her faith in the legal system if she did not make a change. So she went into private practice and quietly accepted more and more pro bono cases. "They don't help feed my husband and daughter," she said, "but they keep me in touch with my Christian values."

That wasn't the end of Kathy's discernment process. Successful as she had been in private practice, Kathy continued to allow the six lamps of revelation to enlighten her and help shape her evolving and deeper yes to being a coworker for the kingdom. She now has given up the practice of law and is enrolled in graduate studies in Christian ethics. Her dream is to teach future lawyers how to practice law with the highest ethical standards.

As disciples of Jesus, we commit to the community of believers called the Church and root ourselves in Scripture and Sacred Tradition. Aided also by prayer and the sacraments, we grow in a deepening appreciation of our identity and mission. That appreciation blossoms when we discern our unique and individual contribution to being a coworker with Christ in realizing God's dream of the kingdom. Like Kathy's, our yes is rarely static; it evolves and grows deeper as we find ourselves in new times and circumstances.

■ REFLECTION QUESTIONS

1. How have your Christian identity and understanding of mission grown over the years? What is the distinguishing hallmark of your current and more mature understanding?

2. Name at least three practical ways in which you have been shaped and transformed by Scripture, the teachings of Jesus, Sacred Tradition, your church affiliation, the celebration of the sacraments, and personal prayer. Of the six lamps of revelation, which one do you consider the most important? The least important? Why?

3. How do you currently see yourself as a coworker with Christ? In what practical ways are you keeping God's dream alive on a daily basis?

CHAPTER 2

TEN ATTITUDES FOR DISCERNMENT

■

The six decades of my life have taught me that discernment is not easy. The process of coming to an awareness of my Christian identity, my mission, and how I could use my gifts and talents to help promote God's long-range plan was slow and gradual—as slow and gradual as the 3,120 weeks it takes to live for sixty years. And just when I thought I had discovered my unique contribution that would take me to my final days, my yes would morph into something deeper and bring a smile of surprise to my face. My evolving yes started with becoming a Franciscan friar and being ordained a priest; it continued with earning a PhD for the purpose of becoming a professor; it mutated into becoming a preacher, a missionary to China, a writer, a college professor, an HR director, and a teacher of future spiritual directors. Who knows what tomorrow might ask of me?

Because our yes evolves and deepens over time, as we are illumined by the lamps of revelation and grow in the understanding of who we are and what we are living for, we need to bring ten attitudes to the practice of discernment. The spiritual tradition reminds us that these time-tested principles ensure creativity and insight as we try to discover the roles we can play as coworkers with Christ.

1. Keep your ears to the ground
and not in the clouds.

I used to think the call of God came from above and was otherworldly. I had to comb the sky for signs and messages from God. I assumed that sooner or later the clouds would part, and I would hear a big, booming voice. Discernment involved gazing heavenward and, like a Marine, being prepared to respond at a moment's notice.

It didn't take me long to see my mistake. God, in fact, invites and speaks in the nitty-gritty of life: in the person needing assistance, the friendship with a neighbor, the contentment felt after a full day's work, the twinge of conscience, the creative thoughts that seem to come out of nowhere, and the frustration with a teenager. My life is the megaphone through which God speaks to me and the world. That's why it's important to keep my ears to the ground and listen to my circumstances.

Luke 18 begins with the parable of the unjust judge and widow. A widow persistently hounds an unjust judge to have justice rendered. The judge refuses until finally, because she keeps nagging him, he relents and issues a judgment.

Scripture scholars tell us that a parable is opened to a variety of interpretations depending on the "take" of the hearer. Luke himself interprets the parable of the unjust judge and widow as the "need to pray always and not to lose heart" (Lk. 18:1). But is God really like the unjust judge who needs to be nagged, harassed, and badgered? I sure hope not.

What if we think of ourselves as the judge and God as the widow who every day comes to us and asks something that only we can do? That's why discernment is a cooperative venture between God and us. That's the story of Gabriel's annunciation to Mary—and that's another way to interpret Luke's parable. How do we hear the invitation of the divine widow? By keeping our ears to the ground and listening to our own lives.

At day's end, it's time well spent to ask yourself: *What is God up to in my life? What is God the divine widow asking of me in the events of today, in this situation, in these feelings or these intuitions?* A reflective, listening stance goes a long way in discovering and shaping your evolving and deeper yes.

2. Use your peripheral vision.

A common discernment mistake is approaching a particular situation wearing blinders, like those sometimes seen on race horses. With tunnel vision, we focus exclusively on the center of our gaze and think only in terms of a yes or no decision. Such a narrow-minded perception of a particular situation cannot include the possibilities that God's grace affords. Mary's vision seems to have been impeded initially when she asked Gabriel, "How can this be, since I am a virgin?" (Lk. 1:34).

Good discernment requires peripheral vision and dreaming of all potential possibilities, options, and alternatives not found right

> If I were to wish for something, I would wish not for wealth or power but for the passion of possibility, for the eye, eternally young, eternally ardent, that sees possibility everywhere.
>
> —Søren Kierkegaard[5]

smack in front of you. Peripheral vision can catch glimmers and glimpses of God's grace that might not be in the center field of focus. As Gabriel told Mary, "[N]othing will be impossible with God" (Lk. 1:37). That's wisdom from the periphery!

Angie and Brian discovered that being broad-minded and thinking "outside the box" can unleash creativity. It opened them to the unexpected. Both from large families, they dreamed of having five or six children after their marriage. Though they were devastated to discover their infertility, the news didn't hamper or impede them. They used their peripheral vision, dreamed about other possibilities, and acted on creative alternatives. Now, after twenty years of marriage, they have fostered fourteen children.

3. Bring a blank check.

God had an excruciating and inscrutable request for Abraham: the sacrifice of his son, Isaac (see Gen. 22:1–19).

Sometimes we reach a point at which we know that if we go any further, we will either lose our faith or break through to a new dimension of faith that goes beyond creedal believing to authentic personal trust. Like Indiana Jones, we come up to the edge of the abyss, and there is no bridge. Only when we step out with one foot into the yawning chasm of unknowing does the bridge appear.

—Margaret Silf[6]

Contemporary readers squirm and are mystified as Abraham, without question or hesitation, responds and emerges as the preeminent model of generous obedience.

Mary is an example of another kind of generosity. As I mentioned in chapter 1, in first-century Judaism, women could own no property. So the only thing a woman could call her own was her reputation. And yet, it was precisely her reputation that God asked Mary to sacrifice in the story of the Annunciation. And Mary freely offered it to God.

Are you willing to respond to any request of the divine widow, or do you put conditions on God and limitations on your response? Discernment requires Abraham's generosity and Mary's indifference to the ego. It dares us to be unrestrained and unconstrained. It challenges us to avoid the tightfisted attitude of a cheapskate who puts God on a budget and says, "I'm willing to do whatever you invite me to do as long as you don't ask me to move my family, look foolish, or change my career path." Without a wholehearted, magnanimous response, our discernment could be flawed.

4. Don't bring any baggage with you.

I remember being six years old and paging through a Catholic magazine. I saw a picture of a Franciscan friar, dressed in the white missionary habit, riding on an animal as he crossed a river in China. I can distinctly remember saying to myself, "That's what I want to be when I grow up! A Franciscan missionary to China!"

Never in my wildest dreams did I ever think that was going to be a possibility. And then, in September 1991, the Rome-based General Minister of the Franciscan Order sent out a request asking if any of the 17,000 friars of the world would be interested in volunteering for a renewed missionary endeavor to mainland China. I knew I had to respond—but I initially didn't. I was in the troves of building a successful preaching career and enjoying all the adulation and fame that came with it. It would take a number of months before I could free myself from the ego to respond with my yes.

The ego is a heavy piece of luggage that slows us down on the spiritual journey and in the process of discernment. Its attachments, biases, preoccupations, and fears often hinder us from offering God a deeper yes. What's in it for me? Will I look foolish, and will people think me crazy? Will I feel satisfied? Will I have enough to live on? These questions of the ego cripple our openness, generosity, and peripheral vision. Self-centeredness is the bane of authentic discernment.

Discerning our unique contribution to God's dream requires an interior freedom from the ego's obsession with self-concern, self-image, self-gratification, and self-preservation. The Chinese word for "intelligent" or "bright" (慧) offers us an insight. It consists of two pictograms: at the top is the word for broom (扫); the bottom is the word for heart (心). The intelligent or bright person has the heart swept clean of ego attachments. Blessed, indeed, are the clean of heart (see Matt. 5:8).

5. Keep your eye on the ball. Don't get sidetracked with circus sideshows.

The one priority of discernment is to respond with a wholehearted yes to whatever invitation the divine widow places before us. That is the animating desire out of which a Christian lives; that's the ball we want to keep our eye on. Discernment demands keeping priorities straight.

There's always a temptation to give more importance to the superfluous and trivial in our lives. The desires of the ego and creature comforts—what I call "circus sideshows"—can be so enticing, attractive, and alluring.

I initially hesitated to respond to the call to China because of "my" preaching ministry. I was serving my own ego in a quest for the circus sideshow of fame. Now, having returned from China after more than a decade of missionary activity, I am back preaching as I had done before I left, but I truly believe it's now about being a coworker for the kingdom and not about gaining notoriety.

Jesus says, "No one can serve two masters" (Matt. 6:24). We must choose between God's dream of the kingdom or the ego's agenda with its obsessions. In this light, St. Ignatius of Loyola offers a practical spiritual exercise to keep our discernment process honest. Using imagery from his early life as a soldier, he asks us to consider the question: Under whose standard are you standing, marching, and fighting? God's? The devil's? Your own? In other words, whose side are you really on?

6. Be a lion with the heart of a lamb.

Do not lose heart, even if you should discover that you lack qualities necessary for the work to which you are called. He who called you will not desert you, but the moment you are in need he will stretch out his saving hand.

—St. Angela Merici[7]

Saying yes to a divine invitation can be difficult, excruciating, and even risky. Consider again the examples of Abraham and Mary. But our response is always rooted in God, whose voracious enthusiasm—what we call grace—keeps us where we are called. God neither asks the impossible nor violates our commitments and responsibilities. The spiritually mature are well aware that God's grace shapes the contours of their courage and bravery.

The lion's courage, paradoxically, is tempered with the heart of a lamb. Lambs are prodded along and led. That's why discernment also involves surrender and trust—two stances that emerge as we come to a deeper understanding of what it means to be a disciple of Christ and a coworker for the kingdom. The last words of the risen Christ to Simon Peter are well worth noting: "Very truly, I tell you, when you were younger, you used to fasten your own belt and to go wherever you wished. But when you grow old, you will stretch out your hands, and someone else will fasten a belt around you and take you where you do not wish to go" (John 21:18). That's what it means to walk by faith, not by sight (see 2 Cor. 5:7).

I ended up living as a missionary in mainland China for eleven and a half years. In October 2003, I began being followed by the Chinese Security Police, in the capital of Beijing. I had lived in China long enough to know that once the Security Police begins to follow you, it's only a matter of time before they show up at your door, give you twenty-four hours to pack, and then expel you from the country. Fearing the clock had started ticking and my time was running out, I immediately flew back to the United States to discuss the situation with my religious superiors. After a day of prayer, reflection, and discussion, we decided it would be best for me to move from Beijing to another city in China and start my ministry again from scratch.

As I flew on the thirteen-hour flight from Chicago to Beijing, I suddenly heard a voice speaking to me. "Albert, it's time to end the adventure. It's time to go home for good." I was stunned and surprised. I tried to ignore the voice but was unsuccessful. I started protesting. If I returned to the States, what would I do? Wouldn't it be a wasteful sin after spending so much time, energy, and money learning a new language and culture? Wouldn't the friars look upon me as a failure?

While I had the lion's courage to move to another city and start all over, I initially didn't have the lamb's heart to say yes to a divine invitation requiring surrender and trust. But after returning to China and wrestling for more than six weeks with what I considered to be a divine invitation, I gave in and began packing up. I had decided to return to the States, though I had no idea of my discernment's ramifications.

The account of Gabriel's annunciation to Mary concludes, "Then the angel departed from her" (Lk.1:38). With the courage of a lion and the heart of a lamb, Mary was momentarily left alone with the consequences of her yes and the challenge to walk by faith.

7. Adopt the turtle as your mascot.

The discernment and discovery of our unique contribution to God's long-range plan require self-knowledge, self-reflection, and introspection. Just as a turtle retreats into its shell, so we need to go within to ponder, consider, and contemplate options and possibilities. But too much "shell time" can devolve into a crippling form of self-absorption.

Discernment also requires that we stick our heads out of the shell and look around. Read the signs of the times and the handwriting on the wall. What is the required duty of the present moment? What are the unmet needs requiring attention? Required duties and unmet needs are most revelatory of what God the divine widow is asking right now.

There is no shortcut or fast track to the process of discernment. Though there are times when you want to go at a rabbit's speed, only the turtle's pace allows clarity to unfold in its own way. Hasty discernments can lead to harmful decisions. When a situation does, in fact, call for a quick response, however, go within, look outside, and then put one foot forward, trusting God's pleasure in any decision made in good faith.

8. Be aware of your desires; don't beware them.

With the birth of her twins, Alice left a teaching career to become a stay-at-home mom. Now that those children were college freshmen, she found herself bored and restless. She began thinking about possibly returning to the classroom. A door of opportunity opened, and a wonderful offer to teach part-time at a local community college presented itself. "I really would love to accept this job offer," she told me. "It's the right fit. I'm just not sure if this is what *God* wants."

There is a strain in pseudo-Christian spirituality that is suspicious and distrustful of personal wishes and individual desires. Some people set up a false dichotomy between "my desires" and "God's will," suggesting the two mutually contradict one another. They think, if I want it, it certainly can't be of God. Or maybe, God's will is like medicine: it always tastes bad to the patient.

St. John of the Cross reminds us that nothing could be further from the truth. God communicates to us precisely through the attractions of our heart. What we experience as a deep, recurring desire could very well be an invitation from God to be a coworker for the kingdom; it could be the word of God yearning to be born and made flesh in our lives.

This, of course, can be tricky since the heart is sometimes in the clutches of the ego with its obsessions over self-concern, self-image, self-gratification, and self-preservation. That's why it's important to travel light and to keep your eye on the ball.

9. Walk the tightrope between the head and the heart.

Some people think through a decision cerebrally, basing it on reason, good judgment, logic, and common sense. But they soon discover that some decisions, though they make all the sense in the world, can be ill-advised and dangerous. Other people, like me, prefer to feel their way to a decision based upon emotion and the gut reaction to a situation. But we, too, discover that even though a decision feels right, it can throw us totally off kilter.

In either case, the time-tested advice for striking a careful balance is well worth remembering: Thinkers should "trust your head but use your gut," and feelers should "trust your gut but use your head." Good discernment incorporates reason and emotion in the decision-making process.

10. Make it a family affair.

Discernment is never a solitary affair. It includes dialogue and discussion with the people who will be affected by any final decision. Have you brought the situation to the dinner table? Have you talked about it over coffee with friends and neighbors? Have you sought the advice and counsel of others who know you well? Don't discern alone and in private; the effects could be disastrous.

The discernment process also includes leaning on another partner for guidance, counsel, and direction: the Holy Spirit. As a baptized believer committed to keeping God's dream alive, I spend time in prayer. Prayer's lamp of revelation illumines my role in salvation history and reminds me that discernment is more than making a good decision; it's ultimately about saying yes to the invitation of the divine widow.

As the six lamps of revelation enlighten our understanding of Christian discipleship, we find ourselves growing spiritually and getting better at keeping our ears to the ground, writing God a blank check, becoming a lion with the heart of a lamb, keeping our eyes on the ball in freedom, paying attention to deep-seated and recurring desires, and walking the tightrope between the head and the heart while soliciting the advice of others. Without discernment, discipleship remains superficial with no personal investment. Without discipleship, discernment is mere decision making. Discipleship and discernment go hand in hand.

■ REFLECTION QUESTIONS

1. When was the last time you experienced God the divine widow inviting you to do something? How did you respond?

2. Which circus sideshows grip your heart and prevent you from offering God a wholehearted yes? How can you sweep your heart clean and grow in interior freedom?

3. Are your decisions based more upon reason, common sense, and logic, or upon emotions and gut reactions? How has your decision-

making process served you in the past? What role, if any, has your Christian discipleship played in it?

CHAPTER 3

LISTENING: THE HEART
OF DISCERNMENT

■

Discernment is discovering how to respond uniquely to the divine widow's invitation to be a coworker for the dream of God's kingdom. That response isn't just plucked out of thin air; nor is it a static, once-in-a-lifetime decision. Rather, our yes arises, emerges, and evolves as we are illumined by Scripture, the ministry of Jesus, Sacred Tradition, the Church, her sacraments, and prayer. That enlightenment helps us grow in the ten attitudes of a discerning disciple. Discernment, like our understanding of Christian discipleship, is an ongoing and lifelong process.

How do you know when God is inviting you to contribute to salvation history? How do you know when to say yes? When does a situation call for a deeper yes? Answering these questions lies at the heart of the discernment process; it requires listening to your life, the megaphone God uses to communicate with each of us.

There are ten speakers that offer a grace-filled wisdom unique to our personal relationship with God, others, and self. Their wisdom and experience are invaluable aids not only in hearing the divine widow's request, but also in discovering our emerging, evolving, and deeper yes. Taken together and given attention, they also help indicate the best time to respond. Let's take a look at each speaker and what it can tell us as we discern our identity and mission.

The Past

One's upbringing, place in the sibling pecking order, family finances, academic education, and social interactions lay the foundations for one's personality and future opportunities. The youngest and only daughter of six children, Marge was always told she was "special"—and now, as an adult, she expects to be treated as such. Don has eight siblings and consequently enjoys working in large groups, while Phyllis is an only child and is comfortable working alone. Carol's advanced education nourished her appreciation for the fine arts. Phil internalized childhood memories of being teased on the playground; consequently, he struggles with issues of self-esteem and self-worth. For better or worse, we are products of our *past*.

In big ways and small, past memories offer cautionary advice: after touching a burning stove a couple of times, a child learns not to do it again; after a number of painful experiences with an acquaintance, I come to discover that the person is toxic to my emotional health; a slew of broken promises and shattered pledges speak volumes about one's spirit of commitment.

The past can also tell us about our present passions and interests. Raised in poverty and a witness to injustice herself, Ruth is passionate about her volunteer work with poor, disadvantaged children. Raised in wealth and a recipient of gratuitous favors, Michael enthusiastically promotes the creative arts in his hometown. The memory of being six years old and seeing a picture of a Franciscan missionary crossing a stream in China was the gasoline that fueled my desire to become a missionary to China.

The past offers insights into who we are, how we got to where we are today, and how God's voracious enthusiasm experienced in grace has touched us. In discerning our role in the cooperative venture with God's kingdom, we listen to the past because it provides the background music for the present.

Hunches and Intuition

One morning while taking a shower, Dennis got the idea of getting involved with a Catholic radio station. This came out of nowhere, and even though he had no past experience in the communications industry, he couldn't shake it off. That started a three-year process of discernment that led Dennis to bring Catholic radio to his college town. At age thirty-eight, his yes had evolved.

Ever have a quirky urge to do something that appears irrational or for which you are totally unprepared? Ever have a funny feeling in your stomach that tells you "something's not quite right"? Ever hear a little voice in your head that steers you in the right direction? God sometimes uses *hunches* and *intuition* to invite our conscious mind to consider or reject a project.

Social psychologists such as David Myers of Hope College explain that the intuitive right brain is almost always "reading" our surroundings even when our conscious left brain is engaged with the business at hand. The body listens and registers these intuitive hunches while the conscious mind remains unaware of what's going on. That's why the quirky urge or little voice arrives seemingly unannounced; like a shooting star, it comes out of the blue and blazes across our consciousness. It's the flash of insight that arises while doing a mindless activity like ironing clothes or walking the dog or taking a shower.

When it's God Who is speaking . . . the proper way to behave is to imitate someone who has an irresistible curiosity and who listens at keyholes. You must listen to everything God says at the keyhole of your heart.

—St. John Vianney[8]

Hunches can be hints of the holy that energize us to boldly proclaim a yes; they can also be God's way of challenging us to pause and ponder again. That is why discerning—which means "sifting through" and "discriminating"—requires listening. Gut feelings, mentally "seeing yourself" doing something, and that nagging inner voice are saying something. To ignore them is to discount what the divine widow might be saying through the right brain.

What's more, the spiritual tradition reveals that responding to spontaneous sympathetic urges toward generosity help bring us out of our egocentricity and often lead to a deeper sense of identity and mission. In his *Testament*, Francis of Assisi said his encounter with the leper changed what previously had been bitter and repulsive to him into a source of sweetness and joy; that began a process of discovering his initial yes that continued to evolve over the next twenty years.

The Body

For almost fifty years, psychotherapists have been promoting the idea that the *physical body* has its own language and even its own memory. Starting with the pioneering work of Eugene Gendlin and his listening technique called Focusing, a whole science of learning and interpreting the language of the body has developed. In recent years, this has progressed into the spiritual practice of mindfulness.

The body speaks in a physical response or reaction. Gendlin refers to it as a "felt sense" or "body sense." It is more basic than emotions. As you ponder your role as a coworker for the kingdom, be aware of what the interior adrenalin surge that fills you with energy is saying. Or the tension in your shoulders. Do you have sweaty palms? Does your yes bring a smile or a frown to your face? A participant in my spiritual director training program jokingly refers to her "loquacious stomach" that is quick to indicate a bad idea.

Mindfulness of the body takes practice. In its simplest form, it requires sitting in a relaxed, comfortable position and mentally attending to your body parts. Starting with your toes and feet, scan your calves to your thighs, through your genitals to your stomach, through your shoulders to your hands and fingers, neck, and head. What is your body saying? The twitch, the knot, the throbbing, the warm feeling, or the cold constriction is offering you wisdom and advice. Does it bring back any memories or feelings from the past that are helpful for your discernment?

Christian spirituality is rooted in the Incarnation: God's Word became flesh. That continues in our own creation as embodied individuals. Consequently, the body has its own advice and does not lie; our challenge is taking the time to listen and interpret what it is saying.

The Imagination

Imagine yourself as a participant in the scenario that could arise from saying yes to an invitation you are considering. Notice your movements and feelings as you visualize yourself in the future and wear its clothing right now. Do you still feel like yourself? Do you feel free? Excited and energized? What do your past, your intuition, and your body say about it? Listen to each speaker as it offers its own wisdom and advice.

God speaks to us through the *imagination*. This is our ability to daydream and fantasize about our future. Like children, we play in the mental attic of tomorrow and try on different visions or versions of ourselves, seeing how we look and feel in them.

In his *Spiritual Exercises,* Ignatius of Loyola, the great master of discernment, capitalizes on the wisdom of the imagination. He suggests three practical exercises. The first is imagining yourself as a trusted advisor to another person who comes to you for advice about the very decision you are facing. Wanting the best for that person, what advice would you offer? What would you encourage that person to do? The second exercise is imagining yourself on your deathbed and noting the joys and sorrows of a lifetime. From that vantage point, what would you like to have said yes to? The final exercise is imagining yourself standing before God at the Last Judgment and asking what you would like your life to have proclaimed.

Because it taps into our creative foresight, imagination has an almost godlike quality. Its advice and wisdom come from beyond the present moment's horizon.

Reason

Some people "think through" decisions. Their decisions are the rational and logical next step in the historical unfolding of their lives; they just make plain old "good sense." As we listen to *reason*, we logically and methodically consider the advantages and disadvantages of what we are considering. Some people find it helpful to make a list of pros and cons on a piece of paper.

Reason weaves the ropes that hinder the hot-air balloon of imagination from taking off into a flight of fancy. And therein lies its gift: it keeps our feet on the ground. And therein lies its curse: it can thwart a unique summons of the Spirit. However, as I hope you are discovering, it is only one of ten speakers God uses to communicate with us.

Feelings

Does your decision produce an afterglow of peacefulness, prayerfulness, and happiness? Is there a wave of rightness about the yes that washes over its initial discomfort? (Remember: some yeses initially might be uncomfortable). Is there a visceral positive conviction that is deeper than just feeling good? Or is there a sense of irritation and agitation that goes against your grain? Does it make you restless, discouraged, heavy, or disinclined to proceed? Does it just feel wrong?

Besides imagination and reason, Ignatius of Loyola stressed a third important speaker: *feelings*. Some people, like me, "feel their way to a decision." We consider feelings a barometer that offers a special kind of input. Others dismiss feelings and have been taught to avoid them when discovering and discerning their deeper yes; like bad weather that is here today and gone tomorrow, they consider them fleeting and fickle. However, the spiritual tradition gives them a place of recognition—as we with reason mull over our yes, we check in with our emotions: How does it feel?

As I discerned my yes to China in the fall of 1991, it made absolutely no sense whatsoever on the level of reason. I was too old and set in my ways to learn how to live in another culture. I didn't have the gift for learning languages. But on the feeling level, despite initial fears, it energized me and felt so right.

In late 2003 when I heard that voice say, "It's time to end the China adventure and return home," I felt sad; but as I pondered it over the following days, it felt right.

As with reason, we approach the speaker of feelings with care, giving it neither too much power and volume nor too little consideration. We honor it as another place where the Spirit speaks to us.

Dreams

Did you know that everyone dreams approximately five to seven times a night? But not everyone remembers the dreams. If a dream is not deliberately called to mind, told to someone, or written down within five minutes after waking, it disappears from memory. *Dreams* can teach, entice, warn, invite, expose, and conceal. Because they are manifestations of the unconscious, their content can provide helpful insights into our response to the divine invitation. But accessing that wisdom is challenging, because everything in a dream is symbolic.

There is no shortcut to dream interpretation. It is hard work. I don't recommend buying or reading books on dream symbol interpretations, because most dream symbols are highly personalized: everything in a dream is about you or some aspect of your personality or situation; even when you are dreaming about other people, you are dreaming about some aspect of yourself that you associate with them.

> A dream which is not interpreted is like a letter which is not read.
>
> —The Talmud

A dream seldom reveals more than we can tolerate knowing or dealing with. As a matter of fact, it often indicates the time to begin dealing with something we might have been unwilling to face. So treat your dream—even the most unsettling of them—as a trusted friend. Especially note recurring dreams that are like flashing neon signs telling you to pay attention to something. Ask yourself some simple questions: *What is this dream about? What is really happening here? What is it telling or teaching or asking me? What is the theme or subject of the dream? What thoughts, feelings, or memories arise when I remember this dream?*

In September 1991, faced with the General Minister of the Franciscan Order's request for volunteers to join the Franciscan Order's China Project, I knew I had to respond, but I initially didn't. I was too obsessed with my ego's lust for fame and success. I also kept telling myself that I was too old to attempt learning a new language and a different culture. However, because of a dream, that inner monologue stopped within months. In the dream, I was in a library. I approached one of the bookcases and was surprised to see all the books were written in Chinese. I pulled one off the shelf. I instinctively opened the book from the back cover where Chinese books traditionally begin and began moving my finger down the page from top to bottom and right to left. I found myself understanding the Chinese characters that I used to refer to as "chicken scratch."

That dream recurred four or five times. As I pondered it and its meaning and message, I understood that I was not too old to learn a new language. I came to realize that my yes to God's kingdom, made once in my discernment to become a Franciscan priest, was now emerging into a deeper yes: I was being given the opportunity to become that missionary to China I had seen in a magazine as a six-year-old boy.

Pay attention to images. Dream wisdom is conveyed through concrete symbols. These images bring us into contact with issues in our unconscious that need to be explained and worked out. Over the years, in times of stress when I am not being attentive to my physical or emotional needs, I've noted that I dream of being strapped to the top of a fast-moving bus or of speeding in a car with broken brakes. These dreams are telling me my life is out of control and needs some balance.

Make conscious associations with the symbols in your dream to help decode its wisdom. Ask yourself: *What is my history with this person, animal, or flower that appears? What does it represent or what past experience does it call to mind?* When I am consciously living a balanced life, I will typically dream of feeling relaxed as I paddle through a Louisiana bayou with its arching cypress trees; it hints to the carefree emotions of my childhood when life was uncomplicated.

The only one who can accurately interpret a dream is the dreamer. A light will come on, sometimes accompanied with a feeling of rightness, as the person realizes what he or she always knew. Family, trusted friends, and spiritual directors can help with the process of interpretation, but it is ultimately the dreamer who makes the final determination whether or not an interpretation is accurate.

These seven speakers require self-awareness, self-knowledge, and introspection. Like our mascot the turtle, we go within our shells and ponder. But the divine widow also invites and advises in the surrounding circumstances in which we find ourselves. Consequently, discernment requires sticking our heads out of the shell, looking around, and listening to three more voices.

Creation

Bernard of Clairvaux once offered this spiritual advice in a letter, "Believe me as one who has experience, you will find much more among the woods than ever you will among books. Woods and stone will teach you what you can never hear from any master."[9] Like any artist, the Creator invites and communicates through the masterpiece of *creation*.

Don't go looking for coded personal messages in the flock of geese flying overhead or in the water stains left on a concrete wall. Rather, following the wisdom of Bernard of Clairvaux, observe nature and prayerfully consider how a particular rock, twig, or bird in all its baffling and mystifying otherness might be analogous to what God is asking of you or to the yes you are considering.

Listen to the sermon preached to you by the flowers, the trees, the shrubs, the sky, and the whole world. Notice how they preach to you a sermon full of love, of praise of God, and how they invite you to glorify the sublimity of that sovereign Artist who has given them being.

—St. Paul of the Cross[10]

Bill is an ordained permanent deacon in the Catholic Church and a participant in my spiritual director training program. He offered a perfect example of how to listen to creation. As a result of being stung multiple times as a child, Bill is skittish around bees and wasps. Feeling overworked, a bit resentful, and out of touch with God, he decided to make a private weekend retreat at a local retreat house. He was wondering what, if anything, God was calling him to in the midst of his hectic and overbooked schedule. During the weekend, he took a walk outside and sat on a bench surrounded by bushes. He suddenly became aware of a cluster of bees frantically buzzing around one of the bushes. Based upon his past experience with bees, he normally would have moved away. But this time something told him to stay put and watch the bees. His observation drew out a thought: their frantic pace mirrored his life and activity of late. He felt like a bee buzzing around. But there was one major difference between him and this cluster of bees. They were not alone; they were working together on their apiarian tasks. And that's when it hit Bill: his frantic, overworked lifestyle might not be the best way to do ministry as a deacon. Like the bees, he needed to enlist others so he wouldn't feel alone or build up more resentment, mistakenly thinking he was the only one ministering at the church. By observing the bees, Deacon Bill rediscovered the importance of working with others in being a coworker for the kingdom. Bees reminded him that God's dream for us is a community affair, not an individual enterprise.

All her life, Sherry has had pets. She's had parakeets, dogs, cats, and even horses. During a spiritual direction session, she told me what each pet has taught her. "Birds teach you to eat only when you are hungry. Dogs are great at reminding you about the importance of unconditional love. Peter, my Persian cat, showed me it's okay to ask for attention and affection when I'm feeling lonely. And my horse reminds me to carry someone along when they need a lift." I could tell Sherry was a wise woman who had studied well the book of creation.

People

As we stick our head out of the shell, we must not forget that the divine widow speaks through other *people*. Our family, friends, trusted colleagues, and faith community know us in ways that we don't always know ourselves, and their perspective can be invaluable in helping us discover our identity and mission. I am amazed at the number of priests and religious sisters who, when asked about the source of their religious vocation, reply, "Because Father So-and-So or Sister So-and-So once asked me to consider it!"

While discerning my yes to the missionary venture to China, I was fortunate enough to talk to a few friars who had been missionaries to China in the 1940s. Their experience and advice were most influential in my own discernment process. Family members and good friends also helped convince me that God was calling. And as I later reflected on the voice that told me it was time to return home, I sought the counsel of a German priest in Beijing, who helped me discern my return to the States.

The spiritual tradition makes it very clear: any discernment done in private or shrouded in secrecy can be counterproductive and faulty. The powers of darkness ply their trade under cover and typically refuse exposure. It makes both practical and spiritual sense to seek the counsel of others.

The Present Moment

As we look around outside our turtle shell, we listen to the duties and responsibilities of the *present moment*. In virtually every situation, nothing is more important than our present obligations. Past decisions, wisely made in good faith, lay the foundations for the lordship of Jesus Christ and our deeper yes. Even past sinful actions can be woven into the tapestry of redemption by our decision to be faithful to their consequential responsibilities.

We sometimes underestimate our present situation with its duties as the place of God's invitation for a deeper yes. The ego is always looking over the fence for the more exotic or heroic place—and sometimes the easier, less stressful place—to build the kingdom. This "geographical cure" is a scam of the ego. God's dream becomes a reality and the kingdom is built right here, right now: in my attentive response to a crying infant, the struggles of providing an income for the family, the way I deal with the feelings of loneliness on a Friday night. All are sanctuaries for a deeper yes.

Sometimes we decide in haste or in isolation without consulting others. We might be less than honest or downright deceptive. We might say yes with an avaricious eye on the obsessions of the ego. Such decisions can sometimes give birth to a situation that is debilitating, unhealthy, abusive, dangerous, or even life threatening. In these situations, we need to revisit and maybe renegotiate our decisions. And so a deeper yes might in fact include an about-face or geographical change. This is why the sifting, differentiating, and sorting of discernment can be humbling and even painful.

Helpful Questions

As we discern our unique response to God's voracious enthusiasm, we listen to these ten speakers. They are the megaphone through which God invites and through which we learn our response. Given our personalities and the situation at hand, we might be more attentive to four or five of these speakers. Though that's usually the case, it's wise to check in with each and every one. Practically speaking, that means asking these or similar questions:

How has my past prepared me or left me unprepared for this possible yes? How is this possible yes a natural consequence of my history?

What do my intuition and hunches tell me about this possible decision? Do my deepest yearnings and desires point to this yes? Can I freely say yes, or are extenuating circumstances forcing me to say yes?

Do I feel an adrenalin surge that energizes me, or does my body tense up as I consider my decision? What's the "felt sense" of this decision?

Can I see myself doing this? What advice would I offer a trusted friend who brings this very situation to me?

Does a yes sit well with me and make sense? What are its pros and cons?

How do I feel about this decision? When I ponder it, does it make me feel excited and happy or nervous and distressed?

What, if any, dreams are manifesting the wisdom of my unconscious?

What are the dream symbols teaching me?

What advice is being offered by my natural surroundings?

What suggestions are my family, friends, and church members making to me? Do they see me doing this? What encouragement and reservations are they raising?

How is this potential yes a natural consequence of my present responsibilities and obligations?

Jesus says, "You will know them by their fruits" (Matt. 7:16). What are the potential fruits of my yes?

How does my possible decision promote the kingdom of peace, love, and justice? In prayer, do I experience Jesus encouraging this deeper yes?

How does this potential yes strengthen my personal commitments, especially to my family and friends?

Over a period of time as we pause, ponder, and pray over a possible request from the divine widow, a response emerges. We will never know for certain whether or not our discernment is right. But discernment is not really about being right or wrong. It's about following the faith and trust of Mary who, perhaps with initial confusion, discerned and responded with her yes. With the departure of the angel, she momentarily stands alone yet confident in her identity and mission. With her courage and conviction, we do the same.[11]

■ REFLECTION QUESTIONS

1. Of the ten speakers, to which ones do you give the most attention? The least attention? Why?

2. What challenges or obstacles have you discovered in listening to your life? How have you addressed them?

3. Think back to a decision that proved to be a mistake. What was faulty in your discernment process? How would the information in this chapter have helped you respond with a more accurate yes?

CHAPTER 4

A DISCERNING LIFESTYLE

■

At the end of a one-day workshop on discernment at a large interdenominational church outside Chicago, a participant raised his hand. "Father," the man said, "this day has been very helpful. I appreciate being reminded of the ten attitudes of discernment that I need to bring to every decision I make as a Christian disciple. I also appreciate the way you noted in a very practical way the ten speakers God uses both to invite us and to suggest how we should craft our yes to the kingdom. But there is something I still don't know."

"What's that?" I asked.

"How do I know *when* God is asking something of me?"

The man's question gave me cause to pause. I stammered and fumbled for an answer. It quickly became evident that after an entire day's workshop on discernment, I had forgotten to address the most basic of questions: How and when do you know the divine widow is asking something?

Ongoing Discernment

As I taxied to the airport to catch my flight home, I reviewed how I had spent the day talking about uniquely responding to God's grace at some major moments of decision making. The Christian's response is illumined by the six lamps of revelation and one's growing identity as a coworker with Christ in keeping God's dream alive. I call this process commitment discernment or Discernment with a capital *D*.

There is another kind of discernment. I call it ongoing discernment. Think of it as discernment with a small *d*. It is less of a specific practice and more of an attitude and orientation that permeates the routines of daily life. Unlike commitment discernment, which occurs at a crossroads in life and has the drama of a drumroll associated with it, ongoing discernment occurs at the kitchen sink and has FM music playing in the background. It's a stance of mindfulness.

"Stay Awake!"

Ongoing discernment is about staying awake and living with awareness and attention. It's a spiritual practice that Jesus himself encouraged (see Matt. 24:42; 24:45–25:13). The earliest-known Christian document, Paul's first letter to the Thessalonians, picks up on its importance (see 1 Thess. 5:6) as does the last book of the Bible, the book of Revelation (see Rev. 16:15). These repeated reminders indicate that a life of discernment with a small *d*—living with awareness and attention—doesn't happen by osmosis; it must be deliberately and intentionally practiced.

Our spiritual practices should broaden and deepen our spiritual mindfulness, called by St. Francis of Assisi "the spirit of prayer and devotion." That's just another way of saying that prayer should make us prayerful—that is, more sensitive to God the divine widow who comes each and every day. That awareness recognizes a divine invitation in the encounter with a homeless person on the street; it calls to mind the presence of God when a delightful breeze blows on my face on a hot summer day; it prompts me to make a phone call to a friend, or pricks my conscience to offer an apology. This is the essence of ongoing discernment: responding to the divine widow's request in the nitty-gritty of daily life. I would like to highlight a few specific techniques for fostering and preserving this spirit of prayer and devotion.

The Daily Check-In

If you have ever spent time in a hospital, you know how doctors and nurses will typically pop their heads into your room and see how you are doing. They have a periodic or daily check-in to take your temperature and blood pressure and see how you are feeling. A *daily check-in*, taken three times a day, might be a good way to begin fostering spiritual mindfulness. When you first wake up in the morning, while brushing your teeth, shaving, or showering, briefly look at your upcoming day as best as you can know it, and ask yourself: *What might God be asking of me today? Where might I be called and challenged to lay a brick for God's kingdom? How can I bring the kingdom characteristics of peace, love, and justice to the business meeting, the playground, or an estranged friend or relative? Where can I be a dream keeper and coworker with Christ today?* In other words, try to anticipate the call and challenges of the day. The purpose of this morning check-in is to reboot your mindfulness and intentionally call to mind the importance of living with spiritual awareness.

If I were called upon to state in a few words the essence of everything I was trying to say both as a novelist and as a preacher, it would be something like this: Listen to your life. See it for the fathomless mystery it is. In the boredom and pain of it no less than in the excitement and gladness: touch, taste, smell your way to the holy and hidden heart of it because in the last analysis all moments are key moments, and life itself is grace.

—Frederick Buechner[12]

At noonday, have another short three-minute check-in and ask: *What is God up to in my life today? What is God doing?* Briefly look over the past few hours and ask: *Where and how has God the divine widow come? What is God asking of me and doing with me?* This is a practical way of calling to mind the first attitude of discernment: keep your ears to the ground and listen to what God is saying through the megaphone of the nitty-gritty. This noonday check-in will sometimes reveal an evolving and deeper yes that God may be asking of you.

Before retiring for the evening, have a final check-in. Ask yourself: *How did I do as a dream keeper and coworker with Christ today? What hindered me from responding to God's invitation as I understood it? Where do I need to be more sensitive and attentive tomorrow?* These three questions will help you be more aware of your ego's enslaving obsession with self-concern, self-image, self-gratification, and self-preservation.

The daily check-in promotes the most basic forms of attention and awareness. It helps us develop the knack for knowing when and how the divine widow may ask something. Sometimes God's megaphone might be the circumstances we find ourselves in or a person who comes to us in need or a suggestion made by a neighbor or even a niggling doubt or twinge of conscience. God has a preferred mode of communication with each of us, and the daily check-in helps us discover what it is.

Praying the News

Listen closely to your ten speakers as you watch the evening news, read the daily newspaper, or check your favorite Internet news sites. Do certain stories move you, offer you intuitive hunches, or generate creative thoughts inside of you? If so, share what you are hearing with Jesus in prayer, and listen to how Jesus feels about it. How does Jesus respond? Ask Jesus what you can do to change what happens in the world. Over a period of time—a day, a week, or maybe even months—you might discern an invitation from God. *Praying the news* sometimes brings to light an opportunity for an evolving and deeper yes.

More than twenty-five years ago, Bridget, watching the evening news, heard about the devastating famine in Ethiopia. She saw footage of hundreds of starving children in a feeding camp. The photographer zoomed in on one little child with hands extended, hoping to receive some food from the photographer. This painful scene bored a hole in Bridget's heart. She began praying for this little boy as a representative of all the starving children of the world. She even gave him a name, Mohammed.

A few days later, while attending daily Mass, Bridget heard the Gospel of the hungry crowd following Jesus and the disciples encouraging Jesus to send the people away so they could go to the villages to buy food. And Jesus replied, "[Y]ou give them something to eat" (Matt. 14:16). That saying of Jesus—a lamp of revelation— suddenly lit up in Bridget's heart the image of Mohammed. And then, at Communion time, she was stunned to discover the very action of Mohammed, his hands extended for food, mirrored hers as she said "Amen" and received Communion.

At that very moment, Bridget heard the invitation of God. Over the months that followed, she responded yes. She obtained an updated passport, the required medical shots, and a plane ticket. Nine months later, she found herself feeding starving children who had crossed over the border from Ethiopia into a feeding camp in Sudan.

Granted: it's a dramatic and almost unbelievable story. But the story of Bridget, my eldest sister, shows how God speaks through the megaphone of our lives and how praying the news can help us hear a divine invitation.

Praying with Scripture

Scripture tells us about God's dream of the kingdom and our challenge to be a coworker with Christ in keeping the dream alive. The teachings and events in the life of Jesus provide the blueprint for our lives. *Praying with Scripture*, at least on a weekly basis, is a great way to deepen our Christian identity and sense of mission. Every year during my annual retreat, I spend time reflecting on the Sermon on the Mount (Matt. 5–7), a great summary of the teachings of Jesus. Don't neglect St. Paul, since he provides practical advice on how we should be living and acting in community.

> Action and contemplation are very close companions; they live together in one house on equal terms. Martha is Mary's sister.
>
> —St. Bernard of Clairvaux[13]

As you work your way through the Gospels and the Pauline letters, ask yourself three transformative questions: *What is this passage saying to my head?* How does it affect the way I think about God, others, and myself? *What is this passage saying to my heart?* How does it move me and shape the contours of my love, forgiveness, and compassion? And finally, *what is this passage saying to my hands?* How am I being called to respond? What is the evolving and deeper yes that might be emerging? As you ask these questions, keep in mind the ten attitudes of discernment, and listen to the ten speakers of your life.

St. Augustine of Hippo, the great fourth-century theologian, was transformed by praying with Scripture. He tells us about his moment of conversion in Book 8 of his autobiography, *The Confessions*. In July 386, at the age of thirty-one, Augustine was in the garden of his home in Milan. He had already lived a sexually active lifestyle and produced an illegitimate child. He was restless, had begun reading the letters of St. Paul, and was considering converting to Christianity. On this particular day, while sitting under a tree, he heard a childlike voice telling him to "take up and read." He took this as a divine command to pick up the Bible and read the first passage his eyes fell upon. He opened his Bible at random and read from the letter to the Romans: "[L]et us live honorably as in the day, not in reveling and drunkenness, not in debauchery and licentiousness, not in quarreling and jealousy. Instead, put on the Lord Jesus Christ, and make no provision for the flesh, to gratify its desires" (Rom. 13:13–14). As he meditated on that passage with his head, heart, and hands, he realized what the divine widow was asking. He renounced sex, decided never to marry, and sought to be baptized as a Christian.

Augustine's experience is that of hundreds of thousands of people whose lives have been radically transformed because they responded to the invitation of God in Scripture. Jane was moved to reconcile with a relative after praying with the parable of the Prodigal Son. After losing her husband of thirty-eight years and going into a depression, Lois rediscovered hope as she read how Jesus walked toward the disciples who were struggling in a storm at sea. Andrew occasionally renews his wedding vows to himself as he reads Paul's description of love. On a daily basis, the Word of God takes on flesh in the lives of many Christians committed to praying with Scripture.

Weekly Church Worship

When I walked into the Cathedral of St. Joseph in Wuhan, Hubei Province, China, for the Good Friday service in 1995, I was depressed and discouraged. Not only was I struggling with culture shock, but I was also discouraged by my teaching in the university. As the service began, I was wallowing in a pity party.

Part of the Catholic commemoration of Good Friday is the invitation to come forward and individually venerate the cross of Christ with a kiss. Before doing so, Bishop Dong turned to the congregation and said, "Please remember: as you come forward to kiss the cross, you are not simply venerating the wood upon which Jesus died for your sins. You are also venerating your own personal cross that God has asked you to embrace as a disciple." I watched, mesmerized, as elderly Chinese Catholics who had lived through the shame and suffering of the Cultural Revolution came forward one by one. Each with valor and loving tenderness kissed the cross. Seeing their faith so publicly exhibited and knowing the suffering most had endured, I felt emboldened to step out of the pew and make my way up the center aisle. As I knelt and kissed the wood of the cross, I thought of my struggles with the Chinese culture and the classroom. As I stood up and returned to my pew, I felt the support and encouragement of a community who had suffered so much more than I could ever imagine. In that moment and because of that community worship service, I whispered my yes again to the invitation of God to serve the kingdom in China.

We are not meant to build the kingdom alone. Falling into that mind-set typically devolves into either a pity party or building a kingdom for one's ego. It's in the *weekly church worship* with other believers that we are challenged to forgive and serve others. It's also in the Sunday gathering that we listen to the wisdom of our elders as well as others who sometimes offer new insights. From the earliest days of Christianity, the gathering of the community—"where two or three are gathered in my name" (Matt. 18:20)—has been a privileged place where Christ continues the revelation of God's long-range plan for all creation. As we offer worship and praise to the Father, we also listen deeply to the movements of our soul.

Spiritual Direction

Addressing questions in three daily check-ins, praying the news and with Scripture, and attending weekly worship with a church community will certainly give rise to thoughts and feelings that could possibly be an invitation from God. These thoughts and feelings are the material we bring on a monthly basis to a *spiritual director*. Having a spiritual director is a critical aspect of a discerning, reflective life.

The word *director* is a misnomer because a spiritual director does not really "direct" or take charge of another's life. Nor is the director simply a soul friend with whom a person has a faith-filled conversation. Rather, an experienced spiritual director uses wisdom and experience to ask open-ended questions that direct a person's attention to any potential or emerging invitation from God. Over time, the directee

We need a guide, a
director, a counselor
who helps us to
distinguish between
the voice of God and
all other voices coming
from our own confusion
or from dark powers far
beyond our control.

—Henri Nouwen[14]

grows in the *awareness* of the divine widow, in the ability to talk about the personal experience of God's voracious enthusiasm (*articulation*), and in the facility to *act* upon God's grace. This threefold result enhances the person's Christian identity and mission. Spiritual direction fosters ongoing discernment through dialogue.

The Annual Retreat

We all live enmeshed in real or virtual relationships that pull, tug, and take us in different directions. We are distracted with computers, smartphones, tablets, and iPods. We develop habits and attitudes that often hinder us from the deep listening that ongoing discernment requires. The *annual retreat* unplugs and disengages us from our daily routines: for a period of three days and two nights, we break away from the ego props and diplomas that make us feel important; we dismantle the scaffolding that holds us up and often distracts us. We go into the solitude and silence of the retreat to listen deeply to the events of our life and to discern the call of the Spirit in them.

Some people, intimidated by three days and two nights of silence and solitude, will ask me: What do I do when I am on retreat? I suggest starting by relaxing and decompressing. Take a nap. Take a walk. Spend some time in prayer. Do whatever helps to get the dust in your life to settle.

At some point during your retreat, spend time looking over the past year. What have you learned about God, the significant people in your life, and yourself? Sometimes pondering that question, perhaps even writing about it, will help you become attentive to an emerging and deeper yes God is asking of you.

Ask me not where I live or what I like to eat. . . . Ask me what I am living for and what I think is keeping me from living fully for that.

—Thomas Merton[15]

Before leaving a retreat, it's wise to have a takeaway that will guide you in the coming year. So ask yourself three important questions: Based upon what I have learned about God, others, and myself as I reflected on the past year, *what do I want to start doing? What do I want to stop doing? And what do I want to do with greater intentionality?* In many ways, these three questions will help shape the contours of your emerging and deeper yes for the next twelve months.

Writing

Two other practices can be helpful in staying spiritually mindful and awake. Not everyone finds them worthwhile, so don't feel guilty or think there is something wrong if you find them unhelpful or bothersome. I offer them as two final practices to help promote ongoing discernment.

The first is *journaling*. I can go months without journaling, and just when I think I have lost interest in it, something happens that makes me want to find a quiet place to write and reflect. In the process of writing, insights about God, others, and myself unfold and shape my identity and sense of mission.

Keeping a spiritual journal is different from keeping a diary. A diary records the *facts* of my life: the who, what, where, when, and whys of my day-to-day existence. In a spiritual journal, I record what I hear in the ten speakers; it contains feelings, hunches, gut impressions, hopes, and dreams.

Some periods in life might call for daily journaling; others might call for weekly, monthly, or even seasonal writing. It's important to discover the personal frequency and individual rhythm that work best. Let journaling serve you; don't become a slave to it.

Write honestly and naturally, be it quickly or deliberately. You don't have to write eloquently or even in complete sentences; after all, you're writing for yourself and not for an audience. Don't allow the inner critic to edit or delete anything considered inappropriate. This kind of openness, vulnerability, and honesty breed divine revelation and self-revelation.

What do you write about? Simply reflect upon questions such as these: *What is going on in my life right now, and how do I feel about it? What is God the divine widow asking of me? What am I hearing in the ten speakers? What is the evolving and deeper yes emerging inside me? How and why am I fighting against God's invitation?* Journaling about such questions is a practical tool for living a discerning lifestyle.

Some people remind themselves of their commitment to a discerning lifestyle by writing a *rule of life*. Far from a list of dos and don'ts or a rambling litany of overcommitments or unmet ideals longing to be fulfilled, this is a one-page reminder of the practical ways a person plans to keep ears to the ground and listen to the megaphone of the nitty-gritty. To use a different metaphor, it functions as a trellis of practical exercises upon which a person grows the basic attitudes of ongoing discernment: awareness, attention, and spiritual mindfulness. Many people find it helpful to review and, if necessary, revise their rule of life seasonally or annually.

Living with the spirit of prayer and devotion is not easy for any of us. It challenges us to be deliberate and intentional about listening for God the divine widow even when we are distracted and consumed with the noise of daily living. In practicing techniques that foster ongoing discernment and spiritual mindfulness, we come to discover just how important each one of us is in God's long-range plan for glorious living: salvation history.

▪ REFLECTION QUESTIONS

1. On a scale of one to four, how would you rate your own level of spiritual mindfulness on the average day? When are you more attentive to God? Less attentive to God?

2. Which techniques of ongoing discernment mentioned in this chapter do you currently practice? How do they help foster your own spirit of prayer and devotion?

3. Which techniques of ongoing discernment mentioned in this chapter have you never before considered? How realistic is it to incorporate them in your relationship with God?

CHAPTER 5

DISCERNING THE DESIGNS
OF THE DEVIL

■

The six lamps of revelation enlighten our identity and mission. As we adopt the ten attitudes of discernment and grow in spiritual mindfulness by reflecting and listening to our lives, our sensitivity to the divine widow's invitation is heightened. Our unique contribution to the kingdom of God becomes evident in our emerging and evolving yes.

But we have an opponent who employs devious, deceptive, and divisive tactics that make us forget who we are and what we are made for. The New Testament refers to this antagonist as the "evil one" (Matt. 13:19), the "enemy" (Lk. 10:19), the "ruler of this world" (Jn. 12:31), and the "father of lies" (Jn. 8:44). Who is this adversary whom we commonly call Satan or the devil?

"The Un-Person"

The devil has been portrayed in popular art as a creature with horns, pitchfork, and a tail. Though that image captures an aspect of his insidious nature, it hardly does justice to the fragmented, broken creature he really is.

In 1973 Joseph Ratzinger (who later became Pope Benedict XVI) referred to him as "the Un-Person, the disintegration and corruption of what it means to be a person." Ratzinger continued, "It is particular to him that he moves about without a face and that his inability to be recognized is his actual strength."[16] This fallen, faceless Un-Person is endowed with a conniving intelligence and a perverse will. Created good and loved by God, Satan deliberately chose to work against God's long-range plan for our glorious living and to bring all creation under the lordship of Jesus Christ. Destined by this decision to remain irrevocably alienated from God and outside the kingdom's light, he cannot remain at peace with himself but restlessly devises plots to drag all humanity away from God and into his thick, suffocating, egotistical darkness.

"The Works of the Flesh"

Sometimes, when we see the troubles, difficulties and wrongs all around us, we are tempted to give up. It seems that the promises of the Gospel do not apply; they are unreal. But the Bible tells us that the great threat to God's plan for us is, and always has been, the lie. The devil is the father of lies. Often he hides

How does the devil accomplish his mission? His associates and ways are legion. In Galatians 5, Paul highlights one way: Satan and his demons prey upon the obsessions of the ego in hopes we will choose an alienated life in darkness. The apostle enumerates fifteen "works of the flesh" found in Satan's bag of deception. Though not exhaustive, the list exposes some of the devil's typical ruses and schemes. Let's explore this list with the help of Eugene Peterson's paraphrase found in THE MESSAGE.

his snares behind the appearance of sophistication, the allure of being "modern," "like everyone else." He distracts us with the promise of ephemeral pleasures, superficial pastimes. And so we squander our God-given gifts by tinkering with gadgets; we squander our money on gambling and drink; we turn in on ourselves. We forget to remain focused on the things that really matter.

—Pope Francis[17]

Fornication

Paul begins his list with *fornication*, paraphrased by Peterson as "repetitive, loveless, cheap sex." In its most basic meaning, fornication is sexual relations between two people who are not married or any form of adultery. It fixates on the emotional, physical, or genital dimensions of a relationship without the commitments to lifelong fidelity and selfless sacrifice. The evil one uses all kinds of mental gymnastics to justify and rationalize this heartless grinding of bodies. So the "liar and the father of lies," as Jesus calls the devil (Jn. 8:44), fuels our obsession with lustful self-gratification by persuading us to say more with our bodies than we are willing to commit to with our lives and hearts. That's the lie of fornication: it's hollow sex.

Impurity

A very successful businessman, married with three children, turns his computer on late at night and assumes a whole different identity and personality in Internet chat rooms. His flimsy rationalization? "I'm not hurting anyone." As fornication deceives, *impurity* divides. It alienates us from our true selves and splits us into multiple personalities, some of whom live an illusion and lie. That fantasy can inflict a deep wound.

THE MESSAGE refers to impurity as "a stinking accumulation of mental and emotional garbage" that turns our minds into dumpsters. Seduced by pornographic images and inappropriate personal disclosures, our minds are trashed as we begin viewing and talking with other people as targets of our sexual desires rather than real persons with names and histories. In depersonalizing others, we become animals void of conscience.

Acts of sexual immorality are often the medications we choose to avoid dealing with past emotional traumas or an empty, lonely life. We mask or run away from the emotional pain through a life of compulsive sex. Immorality obstructs the completion of emotional homework that needs to be done if we are to become healthy individuals.

Licentiousness

Have you ever met someone like Thomas? At age thirty-two, he believes the entire universe has been created to cater to his every whim and wish. He always thinks of himself before the group and does not hesitate to give free rein to his deepest, darkest, and most selfish desires. He's a hedonist on steroids, trapped in *licentiousness* or what Peterson calls the "frenzied and joyless grabs for happiness."

Healthy individuals live with moderation and discipline; they appropriately control selfish impulses and inordinate desires. They know the importance of the greater good and actively promote it, sometimes to the point of denying themselves. The devil, on the other hand, looks for people like Thomas who are emotionally frail and naturally self-centered. Finding such a target, Satan takes them by the hand and leads them down a dimly lit alley to a twisted life of vice, depravity, perversion, salaciousness, promiscuity, and debauchery. Think of the Roman emperor Nero or Adolph Hitler and his Third Reich.

Idolatry

It's so easy to fixate on "trinket gods" (THE MESSAGE), such as power, prestige, or possessions, and to equate happiness with acquiring and keeping them. *Idolatry* is as old as the hills.

We are born with a hole in the heart. That hole is a source of restlessness. The father of lies tricks us into believing something outside ourselves can plug that hole, heal us, and make us happy. So our hearts and bedrooms become bloated and swell with these golden calves, emotional knickknacks, and physical tchotchkes. And like the swollen stomachs of hungry children, they are glaring reminders not of a satiated appetite but of a bottomless pit of hunger.

As licentiousness is a fixation upon desires, idolatry is a fixation on external things as the elixir of happiness. St. Augustine wisely reminds us at the beginning of his *Confessions* that we are hot-wired for God alone, and our hearts will remain restless until they abide in the living God.

Sorcery

On any given Sunday morning, turn on your television and surf the channels. Inevitably you will hear a televangelist say, "Invest in my ministry, and God will reward you a hundredfold." He'll tickle your ears with news about sensational apparitions and miracles performed. He'll encourage you to buy healing prayer shawls as well as books and DVDs guaranteeing financial success and personal fulfillment. Even in the twenty-first century, "magic-show religion" (THE MESSAGE) and hocus-pocus spirituality are alive and well.

Like any other pseudoreligion, *sorcery* promotes its own selfish agenda instead of the lordship of Jesus Christ. It goes out of its way to guarantee emotional highs, money in the bank, and the health and happiness it claims are a person's destiny on earth. It is the good news without the cross.

He who seeks not the cross of Christ seeks not the glory of Christ.

—St. John of the Cross[18]

A Christian denomination or spirituality that does not have the cross of Christ center stage is bogus. Authentic Christianity blossoms and flourishes in the shadow of the cross; it stresses self-denial, sharing even from your need, accepting suffering, forgiving the betrayer, loving the enemy, and washing the feet of others. Without the cross, Christianity devolves into a circus sideshow of wizardry and witchcraft.

Enmity

Paul's sixth work of the flesh is *enmity*. "[P]aranoid loneliness" (THE MESSAGE) drives some people to harbor hatred against others due to race, color, creed, or sexual orientation. It isolates oneself and marginalizes others through prejudice, racism, sexism, and discrimination. It shatters the spirit of community.

Strife

As the director of human resources for an international accounting firm in Beijing, I often felt I was working in a hothouse of what Peterson calls "cutthroat competition." Colleagues would lie, cheat, and take personal credit for another's work to gain the boss's attention or a promotion. On numerous occasions I was tempted to outshine others and jump ahead of them with stolen ideas. Endemic to corporate culture, *strife* fuels rivalry and reduces colleagues and associates to adversaries and competitors. Like enmity, it is divisive and obsesses over self-concern and self-image.

Jealousy

Eugene Peterson mistakenly paraphrases *jealousy* as "all-consuming-yet-never-satisfied wants." He has confused it with envy.

Jealousy is the fear that a third person is going to take the love of my life away and replace me. It stokes a fatal attraction that convinces me I need my beloved in order to be happy. My beloved becomes an emotional pawn, a trophy, and the third person is depersonalized into a threat, a rival. This feeling is the devil's kindling for domestic violence or crimes of passion.

Anger

Peterson paraphrases the ninth work of the flesh as "a brutal temper." It's wise to remember that there are two opposing kinds of *anger*: the prophet's fire and the devil's workshop.

The prophet's fire fuels the passion of whistle-blowers who stand up and speak out even though they have nothing to gain and everything to lose. It inflames kingdom coworkers to be resolute and uncompromising in promoting God's dream of a world flowering with peace, love, and justice. It propels people to bring society's marginalized front and center, incites deeper relationships, and builds up an authentic sense of community. It sparks the dynamism and zeal of those who practice the Golden Rule.

The devil's workshop, on the other hand, is the debilitating, uncontrollable wrath that makes others walk on egg shells, brings them to their knees, and moves them to tears. It is the arrogant person's anger and the scornful person's ire. It is defensive, divisive, and destructive.

Quarrels

I used to live in a community with Brother Robert. Within a month of moving into this community, I noticed that Brother Robert used sarcasm to keep everyone at a distance and never had a kind word to say about anyone or anything. He also refused to participate in community activities. He was a killjoy, a cranky sourpuss. His negativity inevitably fueled *quarrels* within the community.

Tragically, some people suffer from what Peterson calls "an impotence to love or be loved." Based upon their upbringing or some past experience, they choose to isolate themselves from others and retreat behind walls of derision and cynicism. Their hearts harden due to lack of love and fossilize due to lack of loving. The devil recruits such caricatures of humanity to help divide a family or community.

Dissensions

While I was preaching a retreat for priests, a retired priest confided, "You have to understand: I'm a liberal Vatican II priest, and the bishop is a conservative John Paul II bishop. That's why he and I are at odds and disagree." The evil one continues to creep into Christian communities, entices individuals to dig in their heels, and cunningly causes rifts using personal allegiances to conservative or liberal leaders as the dividing stick.

When we become content and comfortable with "divided homes and divided lives" (THE MESSAGE), we get trapped in *dissensions*. In 1 Corinthians, Paul reminds the community that such a spirit is antithetical to the unity Christ challenges us to have: "I follow Paul. I follow Apollos. I follow Cephas. I follow Christ . . . " (see 1 Cor. 1:12). Such competitive allegiance betrays the working of a demonic hand.

Factions

People with "small-minded and lopsided pursuits" (THE MESSAGE) congeal on occasion into gossipy cliques in the office or neighborhood. You will find these *factions* making snide, cruel remarks about others around the water cooler or in the local bar or café. Pope Francis hit the mark when he called such gossips "Satanic assassins of the good names of others."[19]

Envy

Eugene Peterson misses the mark when he paraphrases *envy* as "the vicious habit of depersonalizing everyone into a rival." That's jealousy.

Envy is the possessive spirit that bears a grudge because I covet what others have or enjoy. I compare myself to them and make judgments based upon their gifts, their talents, or their possessions. I am unaware and ungrateful for the unique gifts, singular graces, and personal blessings in my own life. Satan stirs the pot of envy when I stop being thankful to God.

Drunkenness

Paul's *drunkenness* is Peterson's "uncontrolled and uncontrollable addictions." Our contemporary understanding of addictions is that they are not sins but illnesses. A person cannot be blamed or held culpable for alcoholism or a gambling addiction any more than one is responsible for the flu or a genetic disease. Medical science tells us there are physical predispositions and psychological triggers that a person has no say over. The devil exploits these attractions to his own advantage. Addictions are not freely chosen; they are shackles with locks fashioned from past choices.

An addiction to drugs, alcohol, gambling, or sex begins with a freely chosen act that is consistently repeated. A habit gradually develops. After a while, the repeated action becomes a chokehold around the neck, and the person physically or psychologically needs the stimulus—and that's when the drug, alcohol, or behavior becomes a pair of locked handcuffs. Addiction is the devil's dance that occurs in his prison of personal disintegration.

Carousing

People sometimes come together and form "ugly parodies of community" (THE MESSAGE). A mob mentality develops based upon prejudice and hatred (think of the Ku Klux Klan), a moral sickness (think of the pornography industry), or a lethal mix of religion and politics (think of the Islamic militants of ISIS). The devil's community consists of sociopaths who have no moral compass; it populates the seedy underbelly of society; it binges on *carousing*.

The Deadly Sin of Acedia

Paul's works of the flesh are variations and mutations of what we traditionally call the seven deadly sins: pride (dissensions, factions, carousing), anger (enmities, strife, quarrels), greed (idolatry, sorcery, jealousy), gluttony (licentiousness, drunkenness), lust (fornication, impurity), and envy. Paul's list ends with "I could go on" (THE MESSAGE).

And noticeably missing from his list is the deadly sin of acedia, often misunderstood as sloth or laziness.

Acedia, from the Greek *akedeo*, meaning "I don't care," is spiritual indifference, a result of discouragement and weary resignation to impending failure. It's the feeling of hitting a brick wall that makes us stop doing what we are doing, turn around, and revert to the past. Satan uses this weapon to dampen our longings, thwart our spiritual progress, and enhance his imagined status in the universe.

The fourth-century Desert Fathers and Mothers of Christianity called this ploy the "noonday devil." At the hottest part of the day, the monks would be thirsty and tired. They would begin reminiscing about the comfort of their former lives, tempting them to throw in the towel, give up on the spiritual life, and leave the desert to return home. This sometimes would be accompanied by an inner monologue in which the desert Christians criticized themselves, told themselves they were no good, and contended that it was both insane and prideful to think they could make any spiritual progress. The noonday devil then would blanket them in acedia, the disdain and distaste for all things spiritual.

You don't need to be in the fourth-century desert to experience the devilish discouragement that makes us regress, mistakenly change our course of direction, or deliberately give in and accept failure. I live with a friar who, as a hospital chaplain, brings home stories of

Most anyone who has endeavored to maintain the habit of prayer, or making art, or regular exercise . . . knows the syndrome [of acedia] well. When I sit down to pray or write, a host of thoughts arise. I should call to find out how so-and-so is doing. I should dust and organize my desk, because I will get more work done in a neater space. While I'm at it, I might as well load and start the washing machine. I may truly desire to write, but as I am pulled to one task after another I lose the ability to concentrate on the work at hand. Any activity, even scrubbing the toilet, seems more compelling than sitting down to face the blank page.

—Kathleen Norris[20]

valiant cancer patients who struggle with the side effects of chemotherapy and consequently abandon their treatments. A friend tells me about a person in AA he sponsors who fails to live up to her ideals and stops working the twelve steps. Some caregivers of Alzheimer's patients suffer from compassion fatigue and walk away. A cloistered Poor Clare nun, reading the daily newspaper and feeling overwhelmed and powerless before the tragedies for which her vocation calls her to intercede before God, stops praying for the war-torn areas of the world. Father Jim has prayed a Rosary with a group outside an immigration court every Thursday morning for more than a year and has since stopped, thinking his prayers are ineffective. The faceless noonday devil slithers into the cracked hearts of even the most ardent coworkers of the kingdom.

Desolation

I had just returned home after being on the road for seven weeks of preaching parish missions. Assured that I would be home for one week, I was excited about sleeping in my own bed for six nights! It was a beautiful day in north Texas. I decided to take a long walk and just enjoy the weather and the comfort of being home. I walked alongside Lake Benbrook, suddenly aware that I was singing to myself. I was joyful and upbeat. But then a negative feeling swept over me, and a self-depreciating monologue started: *Why do I spend so much time preaching on the road? I'm wasting my time. I should be doing some kind of ministry that has lasting value and a positive effect on people's lives.* As this inner monologue continued for forty-five minutes, my good mood dissipated. Second-guessing myself, I became discouraged about my ministry.

Ever have a heavy mood suddenly descend upon you and blanket your spiritual enthusiasm or joyful exuberance? The sin of acedia is typically preceded by a temptation that Ignatius of Loyola calls "the spirit of desolation." I call it the devil's mood.

Sometimes as a reaction to something that has us discouraged—or sometimes out of the blue, as happened during that afternoon walk of mine—the devil's mood, the spirit of desolation, rolls in like a fast-moving storm. Its dark, rumbling clouds turn us in on ourselves and drive us into negative feelings. Not to be confused with "feeling blue," which we all experience on occasion, desolation fogs our vision, drains our spiritual energy, cuts us off from relationships, and tries to draw us away from our contribution to God's kingdom. This faceless demon can sweep over us momentarily or hang over us for a few days.

When experiencing the devil's mood, we need to turn to God and ask for help. Ignatius encourages us to increase our spiritual practices even though that goes against our grain; we might add fifteen minutes to our prayer, have a fast day, or give alms of our time, talent, or treasure. He suggests intentionally strengthening our relationships by seeking out companions or responding with attentive care to someone in need. Finally, Ignatius wisely recommends remaining faithful to our commitments to God, others, and self; he says this is not the time to make or change any important decision. Such responses make the demon scamper away with its tail between its legs.

A discerning lifestyle includes examining one's conscience and admitting one's complicity and guilt in living according to the works of the flesh. Those fifteen works promote the deceptive and divisive agenda of the powers of darkness. Acedia and the spirit of desolation cause spiritual paralysis. By confronting these devilish schemes head on, we hinder the father of lies from sabotaging our deeper yes to God's dream of the kingdom.

■ REFLECTION QUESTIONS

1. In what situations do you find yourself most vulnerable to temptation and sin? When and how have you rationalized or justified a sinful action?

2. Review Paul's fifteen works of the flesh. Of which ones are you currently guilty? What can you do to break the devil's insistence that you continue with them?

3. When was the last time you experienced the spirit of desolation? How long did it last? What did you do to make it dissipate?

CHAPTER 6

WRESTLING WITH GOD

∎

Mary Ann is in her early fifties. She's been a successful real estate agent for twenty of her twenty-five years of marriage. Her husband is a surgeon, and their combined income has given them a very comfortable lifestyle.

Recently a desire has flared up in Mary Ann's heart. She feels an attraction to do something for the poor: maybe volunteer in a soup kitchen or do something for underprivileged children. Every time that desire flares up, she immediately throws cold water on it. She fears her husband and friends might think she is trying to be a little Goody Two-shoes. Though the desire keeps returning, Mary Ann manages to quench and dodge it. Like audacious Jacob wrestling with the angel in Genesis 32, Mary Ann is resisting the call of God.

Saying No to God

Nothing is more harmful to a man than his resistance to Grace.

—Archbishop Fulton Sheen[21]

Mary Ann is not alone. All of us on occasion have denied God's request. Our conscience tells us to offer an apology to a neighbor, and yet the ego vigorously refuses. We feel the plight of society's marginalized and do nothing in response. An acquaintance asks for a lending hand over the weekend, and we make up an excuse to say no. Though our hearts protest, we allow family frictions and dissensions to simmer. We deliberately ignore the truth that someone we love has an addiction and needs an intervention. Though we are so aware of who we are in Christ and what we are called to do for the kingdom, we still don't hesitate to say no to the divine widow. Discernment includes discovering when we actively and deliberately ignore or resist an invitation from God. Let's explore some typical techniques we employ.

Denial

The most obvious method is *denial*. We deliberately ignore the elephant in the room by pretending it's not there. This is cloaked in various attitudes and actions. I flatly refuse to admit the immorality of fudging on my taxes. I get defensive and rationalize or justify an unchristian action by saying, "It's my life, and I have every right to do or say as I please." I ignore the most obvious meaning of a scriptural text: "Jesus's challenge to forgive doesn't apply here. The situation with my former spouse is an exception!" Denial is turning a deaf ear to the call illumined by the six lamps of revelation.

Delay

When I returned to the United States, I had no idea what ministry I would assume. When asked by my religious superior what I felt called to do, I replied, "I have no idea, John. I'm happy to respond to whatever need there is. I ask just one favor: I don't want to get back on that never-ending treadmill of traveling and preaching that I used to do."

He replied that there was an opening in the theology department of Quincy University. "With your PhD in theology, Albert, you would be the perfect candidate for the position. So how about you go and apply for that position?"

Before long, I found myself in the classroom teaching theology. As word got out that I had returned to the United States, however, I received more and more requests to preach retreats and parish missions. I had to decline those requests because my ministry was focused in the classroom, and I couldn't keep canceling classes. Frankly, I was happy to be settled in a friary and not on the road living out of a suitcase. "Been there, done that," I would say to myself.

Over maybe six months, as preaching requests kept arriving, it became evident that God was asking something of me. That was confirmed through discernment, in prayer, and with my spiritual director. Just the thought of returning to itinerant preaching felt like a heavy burden. I still remember praying for more than a year and a half, "I'll do anything, Lord, but not that." I knew exactly where I was being called, but I was dragging my feet in response.

We resist responding to God through *delay*. We procrastinate or deliberately choose paralysis over proceeding. We momentarily fiddle with a request and say, "I'm not sure if this is of God, so I will leave well enough alone," and put it on the back burner. Lest our friends think we are a Goody Two-shoes, we dig in our heels and whisper a firm, "Not now." Control freaks stall because they fear discerning the wrong decision; they are afraid of stepping out in faith—and failing even more.

Sabotage

While denial and delay are passive, *sabotage* is deliberate and intentional. It aggressively connives and works against the invitation of the divine widow. There are four typical personalities who highjack God's grace and call.

I remember a spiritual directee who spent more than five years mulling over whether or not to pursue vowed religious life. Or what about the man who has been happily dating the same woman for eight years and is still waiting for the sign that she's "the one" to marry? *Turtles* are saboteurs who take delay to a whole new level by retreating inside their shells and forever mulling over a decision. They subvert God's voracious enthusiasm for the kingdom by choosing paralysis. They do nothing to engage actively and advance the discernment process. They forget that a deep-seated desire or recurring attraction is sometimes the very sign of the divine widow's invitation. Turtles often fear commitment.

Bumblebees highjack the call of God by flitting here and there, getting involved in other people's business, and never taking the time to pause, reflect, and listen to their lives. They are the polar opposite of turtles, because their escape is through activity. Paul calls these people "busybodies" (2 Thess. 3:11).

Sarah fills up her prayer time with readings, pious thoughts, and words, all the while trying to induce uplifting emotions. Her prayer time is one long monologue with the hope that it erupts into praise and joy. Maintaining control and keeping God at a distance, she never gives God a chance to speak or touch her heart. Similar to a circus barker who tries to drum up people's curiosity for a particular sideshow, *prayer barkers* do all the talking in prayer and never pause to do the deep listening that is critical for discernment.

Bishops, pastors, and people in other ecclesiastical leadership roles sometimes become the fourth kind of saboteur. Being the sole interpreters of God's ways, *know-it-alls* put God in a tightly defined box and claim to know exactly how God acts. They won't entertain anything that doesn't match their image or knowledge of God. They forget that grace is sometimes found outside the box and sometimes destroys the very box that confines our nicely defined theologies of God!

Insight from Ed

Ed came monthly for spiritual direction. When I began each session by asking how he was doing, his reply was always the same: "I'm fine. I'm perfectly fine." Once when I tried to elicit his feelings about his wife's Stage IV cancer, he responded, "God is in charge. It's not right for a Christian to be angry with God because God is the boss." He said that as matter-of-factly as he was stating the weather conditions outside.

After that session as I spent time reflecting on what I had heard, it became clear to me that Ed considered anger an inappropriate emotion to express to God. Ed's begrudging resignation, camouflaged as a stance of surrender to the divine boss, was actually a form of sabotage. That discovery led me to an important insight: if a person's relationship with God is continually flat, unnuanced, and lacking in emotion, odds are the person is avoiding God's invitation through denial, delay, or sabotage.

Spiritual transformation doesn't just happen; it requires deep listening, sometimes struggle, and ongoing conversation with the divine widow about our feelings and response, something Ed clearly was not doing. Reflection, dialogue, and prayer will occasionally lead to wrestling with God as we are challenged to let go of control. Surrender and God's grace nourish deeper and deeper forms of spiritual transformation.

Rebellion

And that leads to the fourth—and believe it or not, most successful—technique we use to wrestle with God. It's *rebellion*. We are consciously aware that God is calling us; we know how we are to respond; we are well aware God will get what God wants; we are angry about that and raise a ruckus. I call it the "most successful" technique because it works to God's advantage and our transformation.

There have been too many times in my life as a friar when I have had disagreements with community members. I often end up saying things I instantly regret. Though my conscience immediately urges me to go and apologize, I typically don't. I allow the resentment to fester. The more my resentment festers, the more my conscience urges me to mend the broken relationship. I know that's what I'm being called to do, but I resist. I wrestle with the grace of reconciliation until finally I begrudgingly give in, approach the injured person, and say the humbling words: "I'm sorry. I apologize." It's easier to give in than to keep fighting my conscience.

Any wise spiritual director will tell you: active rebellion is good. It indicates one's relationship with God is dynamic and alive; it also indicates the person is listening at a deep level. The person is wrestling with transformative grace that is both challenging the ego and calling forth a yes that finds expression in deeper forms of trust and surrender.

Denial, delay, sabotage, and rebellion are four typical ways we avoid God or refuse the divine widow's request. I'm certain there are other ways, because everyone resists and wrestles with God in a personal way. We are limited only by the ego's conniving creativity.

That's why the spiritual life requires self-awareness, a reflective lifestyle, and brutal honesty. Trying to self-diagnose resistance is virtually impossible. Even astute and discerning people miss how they are arm wrestling and resisting God's invitation. Good discernment—and the entire spiritual adventure, for that matter—is never done alone. Having a spiritual director or spiritual companion to check in with on a consistent basis and discuss what's going on spiritually is not only a wise decision but also of critical importance for spiritual growth and maturity.

Obstacles to Our Yes

Why do we ignore or resist the divine widow? Part of the reason is fear. Creatures of habit, we fear the new, the untried, and the unknown—so we tenaciously cling to the puny and myopic vision of our lives. Change initially forces us to let go of control, and the loss of that security is frightening. We are afraid that God is asking the impossible of us. We fear failure and a subsequent loss of face. We are afraid of the ripple effects some decisions will have on other aspects of our lives. Fear is the feeling that forces us to freeze, dig in our heels, and resist.

[God] tears us from that which we love wrongly, unreasonably or exces-sively, that which hinders his love. . . . We cry loudly in our despair and mur-mur against God. . . . But he lets us cry and saves us nevertheless. . . . The things for which we weep would have caused us eternal woe.

—François Fénelon[22]

Resistance also arises around the ego's obsession with self-concern, self-image, self-gratification, and self-preservation as well as the emotional need to avoid pain, blame, criticism, disgrace, and loss. God's call and grace challenge us to disengage from the ego and its avoidance techniques. Because we tenaciously cling to the ego and are constantly dodging anything that makes us feel uncomfortable, we are frustrated and anxious.

Dennis is in his forties. He struggles with frustration. That's because, like many men, he's a control freak. He is very careful and methodical, always hesitant to do anything spontaneous lest it make him look foolish. He is obsessed with his reputation and what people think of him.

This became a problem in his marriage. His wife finally had enough and moved out of the house. Before leaving, she gave him an ultimatum, "Either you deal with your control issues, or I'll divorce you."

When I asked him in spiritual direction what God might be saying or asking of him in this situation, he instantly replied, "God has nothing to do with this. My wife is simply overly sensitive." Dennis is now divorced and still unwilling to face the call from God. He continues to live in denial and frustration.

> God whispers to us in our pleasures, speaks in our conscience, but shouts in our pains: it is his megaphone to rouse a deaf world.
>
> — C. S. Lewis[23]

If you try to ignore or resist the divine widow, your ego remains front and center. That has its consequences: like the unjust judge in Luke's parable of the widow, you will feel "bothered" and "worn out" (see Lk. 18:4–5). Such forms of frustration are often signs that transformative grace is calling you to surrender and trust.

When anxious or frustrated, ask yourself: *What is being threatened? Why am I fighting against this call from God? Am I overly concerned about what I will look like and what others will say? Am I overly occupied with feeling good or having enough to live on? Am I fighting against pain, avoiding blame, dodging criticism, or fearing disgrace? What fear is being activated? What is God asking of me?* Such questions in times of anxiety and frustration help raise the issue of resistance to a conscious level; you'll then be able to discuss it with a spiritual director.

The Prayer of Lament

Lord, my God, who am I that you should forsake me? The child of your love—and now become as the most hated one— the one You have thrown away as unwanted—un-loved. I call, I cling, I want—and there is no One to answer—no One on Whom I can cling— no, No One.—Alone. The darkness is so dark—and I am alone.—Unwanted, forsaken . . . I am told God loves me—and yet the reality of darkness & coldness & emptiness

Even before you bring the fear or the ego's issue to your spiritual director, bring it to prayer. Rather than avoid the emotion, pray *from* and *through* your anger, your fear, your disgust, your sense of abandonment. Don't be afraid to yell at God. Raise a ruckus if you must, and continue to wrestle with God! This rebellion and transparency lead to a more authentic relationship with the divine.

This prayer of lament and complaint is firmly rooted in the biblical tradition. Over one-third of the Psalms are prayed from physical sickness (see Ps. 6:3), loneliness and alienation (see Ps. 38:12), is so great that nothing touches my soul.

—Mother Teresa of Calcutta[24]

danger and mistreatment (see Ps. 7:2), and even aging (see Ps. 71:9). The book of Job is written around the question, why do the just suffer? Prophets such as Jeremiah complain to God, "Why is my pain unceasing, my wound incurable, refusing to be healed? Truly, you are to me like a deceitful brook, like waters that fail" (Jer. 15:18). The entire Book of Lamentations is written from the confusion and suffering felt after the destruction of Jerusalem by the Babylonians.

Lamenting reminds us that no emotion is inappropriate to bring before God. Jesus himself turned to it as he prayed Psalm 22 from the cross, "My God, my God, why have you forsaken me?" (Matt. 27:46). Such a prayer actually sings of a deep—and disappointed—confidence in God.

During the year and a half as a university professor when I resisted the call to return to itinerant preaching, I was frustrated and angry. I knew what God was asking, but I just didn't want to respond. I found it disheartening that my spiritual director didn't try to relieve my struggles with pious platitudes or spiritual Band-Aids. As I continued to wrestle with the angel and prayed with agitation and complaints, an emotional shift gradually occurred; I found myself moving toward another yes. That's when I discovered again the power of lament and how rebellion, oddly enough, is transformative: by actively resisting God, my attitude had changed.

The Power of Pain

That's really the foundation of any twelve-step program, isn't it? Pain and frustration arising from rebellion can be transformative, because they cause the emotional shift that leads you to respond to God. But you must hit rock bottom first; the pain must become unbearable. That's why experienced spiritual directors never deny people their pain or ease it with platitudes—what I call "throwing holy water on someone's suffering." You do the butterfly no favor if you help it break out of the cocoon; it needs to struggle if you want the butterfly to fly. As the Chinese say, out of the mud the lotus flower emerges.

Luke 22 shows a very human Jesus in the Garden of Gethsemane. It's one of the few places in the Gospels where we actually hear his prayer. "Father, if you are willing, remove this cup from me" (Lk. 22:42). Luke tells us that Jesus's struggle was so intense that his sweat became like drops of blood falling to the ground (see Lk. 22:44). And yet, in the midst of that struggle, his deeper yes emerges: "Not my will but yours be done" (Lk. 22:42).

It is a paradox in the spiritual life: rebelling and shaking our fists against God in lament prepare the ground and pave the path to deeper faith and trust. Denial, delay, and sabotage may maintain the ego as our life's operating system, but active rebellion wears down the ego with the ensuing frustration. As the divine widow keeps returning, weariness sets in; and then suddenly, out of that mud, the lotus flower emerges—namely, a positive response to the grace of surrender, acceptance, and trust.

The grace of surrender, acceptance, and trust is not easily received. Though our hands are outstretched in times of rebellion and lament, we approach the response of surrender with baby steps, sometimes yelling and kicking and often with fear and trembling. But this shouldn't discourage us. As with Jesus in his Gethsemane experience, we can gain a deeper understanding of our identity and mission in the crucible of fear and in the desert of doubt. In that crucible and from that desert a flower emerges as we say along with Jesus, "Not my will but yours be done." And with that yes, we discover in a whole new way our personal role in salvation history.

■ REFLECTION QUESTIONS

1. When was the last time you found yourself wrestling with God? How was the situation ultimately resolved?

2. What is your preferred method of resisting God's call: denial, delay, sabotage, or rebellion? How does this method make you feel?

3. What emotions do you consider inappropriate to bring before God? When have you recently prayed in lament and complaint?

CONCLUSION

∎

With voracious enthusiasm, God desires to fulfill a long-range plan, decided upon before the world was created, for our glorious living: with and through his Son, we are to be incorporated into God's family and take our place with all creation under the lordship of Jesus Christ. Jesus referred to this dream as the kingdom.

Our baptism reveals to us our identity in Christ: we are called to be "little Christs." It also reveals to us what we are living for: our mission is to keep the dream of the kingdom alive and to make it a reality by lives of peace, love, and justice. Together with Christ, we are coworkers for the kingdom.

Discernment is the process of discovering my unique and free contribution to the kingdom right here, right now. It is not simply a once-in-a-lifetime decision made at a crossroads; it continues as a daily reflective lifestyle continued at the breakfast table. It involves listening to the nitty-gritty details of the circumstances in which I find myself, because that is the megaphone God uses to elicit my free response to the kingdom. Over time as my circumstances change, my yes to the divine invitation evolves and grows deeper. And with every yes, my identity as a disciple, my mission as a coworker, and my contribution to salvation history are rediscovered and reaffirmed.

PRAYERS FOR DISCERNMENT

∎

Steer the ship of my life, Lord, to your quiet harbor,

where I can be safe from the storms of sin and conflict.

Show me the course I should take.

Renew in me the gift of discernment,

so that I can see the right direction in which I should go.

And give me the strength and the courage to choose the right course,

even when the sea is rough and the waves are high,

knowing that through enduring hardship and danger in your name

we shall find comfort and peace.

Amen.

—Basil of Caesarea[25]
(329–379, theologian of Asia Minor and cofounder of communal monasticism in Eastern Christianity)

∎

Lord Jesus, let me know myself and know You,

And desire nothing except only You.

Let me hate myself and love You.

Let me do everything for Your sake.

Let me humble myself and exalt You.

Let me think nothing except You.

Let me die to myself and live in You.

Let me accept whatever happens as from You.

Let me banish self and follow You,

and ever desire to follow You.

Let me fly from myself and take refuge in You,

that I may deserve to be defended by You.

Let me fear for myself, let me fear You,

and let me be among those who are chosen by You.

Let me distrust myself and put my trust in You.

Let me be willing to obey for Your sake.

Let me cling to nothing but only You,

and let me be poor for Your sake.

Look upon me, that I may love You.

Call me that I may see You

and forever enjoy You.

—Attributed to Augustine of Hippo[26]
(*354–430, theologian, philosopher, and Doctor of the Church*)

O Lord my God,

teach my heart this day where and how to see you,

where and how to find you.

You have made me and remade me,

and you have bestowed on me

all the good things I possess,

and still I do not know you.

I have not yet done that

for which I was made.

Teach me to seek you,

for I cannot seek you

unless you teach me,

or find you

unless you show yourself to me.

Let me seek you in my desire,

let me desire you in my seeking.

Let me find you by loving you,

let me love you when I find you.

—Anselm of Canterbury[27]
(*1033–1109, Benedictine monk, philosopher, archbishop of Canterbury, and founder of scholasticism*)

Most high, glorious God,

enlighten the shadows of my heart,

and grant unto me a right faith,

a certain hope and perfect charity,

sense and understanding,

Lord, so that I may accomplish

Thy holy and true command.

Amen.

—F r a n c i s   o f   A s s i s i [28]
(*1182–1226, preacher and founder of the Franciscan Order*)

Dearest Jesus, teach me to be generous.

Teach me to love and serve You as You deserve,

to give and not to count the cost,

to fight and not to heed the wounds,

to toil and not to seek for rest,

to labor and to look for no reward,

except that of knowing that I do Your Holy Will.

Amen.

—A t t r i b u t e d   t o   I g n a t i u s   o f   L o y o l a [29]
(*1491–1556, Spanish priest and founder of the Society of Jesus*)

Govern everything by your wisdom, O Lord, so that my soul may

always be serving you

as you will,

and not as I may choose.

Do not punish me, I beseech You,

by granting that which I wish or ask, if it offend Your love,

which would always live in me.

Let me die to myself, so that I may serve you;

let me live to you, who in Yourself are the true life.

Reign and let me be the captive,

for my soul covets no other freedom.

Amen.

—Teresa of Avila[30]
(*1515–1582, Spanish mystic and cofounder of the Discalced Carmelite
Order*)

O God,

You have created me to do You some definitive service;

You have committed some work to me which You have not committed

to another.

I have my mission.

I may never know it in this life, but I shall be told it in the next.

I am a link in a chain, a bond of connection between persons.

You have not created me for nothing.

I shall do good.

I shall do Your work.

Therefore, I will trust You, whatever I am.

I cannot be thrown away.

If I am in sickness, my sickness may serve You;

in perplexity, my perplexity may serve You;

if I am in sorrow, my sorrow may serve You.

You do nothing in vain. You know what You are about.

You may take away my friends.

You may throw me among strangers.

You may make me feel desolate, make my spirits sink,

hide my future from me,

but still You know what You are about.

— Adapted by the author from words written
by John Henry Newman [31]
(*1801–1890, important figure in the religious history of England and
cardinal of the Catholic Church*)

Father,

I abandon myself into Your hands;

do with me what You will.

Whatever You may do, I thank You.

I am ready for all; I accept all.

Let only Your will be done in me,

and in all Your creatures.

I wish no more than this, O Lord.

Into Your hands I commend my soul.

I offer it to You with all the love of my heart,

for I love You, Lord,

and so need to give myself,

to surrender myself into Your hands,

without reserve and with boundless confidence,

for You are my Father.

Amen.

—Charles de Foucauld [32]
(*1858–1916, French priest and martyr, inspiration for the Little Brothers and Sisters of Jesus*)

Lord, grant that I may always allow myself to be guided by You, always follow your plans, and perfectly accomplish your holy will.

Grant that in all things, great and small, today and all the days of my life, I may do whatever You may require of me.

Help me to respond to the slightest promptings of your grace,

so that I may be your trustworthy instrument, for your honor.

May your will be done in time and eternity—by me, in me, and through me.

Amen.

—Thérèse of Lisieux [33]
(*1873–1897, French Discalced Carmelite nun popularly called the "Little Flower"*)

My Lord God,

I have no idea where I am going.

I do not see the road ahead of me

nor do I really know myself,

and the fact that I think I am following Your will

does not mean that I am actually doing so.

But I believe that the desire to please You

does in fact please You.

And I hope that I will never do anything apart from that desire.

And I know that if I do this,

You will lead me by the right road

though I may know nothing about it.

Therefore will I trust You always

though I may seem to be lost and in the shadow of death.

I will not fear, for You are ever with me,

and You will never leave me to face my struggles alone.

Amen.

—Thomas Merton [34]
(*1915–1968, Catholic writer, Trappist monk, poet, and social activist*)

Dear Lord, the Great Healer, I kneel before You,

since every perfect gift must come from You.

I pray, give skill to my hands,

clear vision to my mind,

kindness and meekness to my heart.

Give me singleness of purpose,

strength to lift up a part of the burden

of my suffering fellow men,

and a true realization of the privilege that is mine.

Take from my heart all the guile and worldliness

that with the simple faith of a child,

I may rely on You.

Amen.

—Mother Teresa of Calcutta[35]
(*1910–1997, Roman Catholic missionary, founder of the Missionaries of
Charity, recipient of the Nobel Peace Prize*)

OTHER BOOKS AND MEDIA BY ALBERT HAASE, OFM

■

Swimming in the Sun: Rediscovering the Lord's Prayer with Francis of Assisi and Thomas Merton

Enkindled: Holy Spirit, Holy Gifts, coauthored with Bridget Haase, OSU

Instruments of Christ: Reflections on the Peace Prayer of St. Francis of Assisi

Coming Home to Your True Self: Leaving the Emptiness of False Attractions

Living the Lord's Prayer: The Way of the Disciple

The Lord's Prayer: A Summary of the Entire Gospel (Audio/CDs)

This Sacred Moment: Becoming Holy Right Where You Are

The Life of Antony of Egypt: By Athanasius, A Paraphrase

Catching Fire, Becoming Flame: A Guide for Spiritual Transformation

Catching Fire, Becoming Flame: A Guide for Spiritual Transformation (Video/DVDs)

Keeping the Fire Alive: Navigating Challenges in the Spiritual Life (Video/DVDs)

Come, Follow Me: Six Responses to the Call of Jesus (Video/DVDs)

Notes

■

1   Pope John Paul II, General Audience, July 13, 1994, as quoted at http://www.faithleap.org/womenessential.htm, accessed September 4, 2015.

2   Hans Urs von Balthasar, *Prayer* (Ignatius Press, 1986), as quoted at http://www.goodreads.com/author/quotes/30796.Hans_Urs_von_Balthasar, accessed September 4, 2015.

3   St. Francis de Sales, as quoted at http://thecatholicreader.blogspot.com/2013/06/holinesssanctity-quotes.html, accessed September 4, 2015.

4   St. Eugene de Mazenod, cited in "Retreat in preparation for the taking possession of the See of Marseilles," in *Oblate Writings*, I, vol. 15, no. 185, p. 238. As quoted at http://www.omiworld.org/en/dictionary/dictionary-of-oblate-values_vol-1_s/1075/sacred-scripture/, accessed September 4, 2015.

5   Søren Kierkegaard, *International Kierkegaard Commentary, Either/Or*, Part I, volume 3, Robert L. Perkins, ed. (Macon, Georgia: Mercer University Press, 1995), 61.

6   Margaret Silf, *Inner Compass: An Invitation to Ignatian Spirituality* (Chicago: Loyola Press, 1999), New Introduction to the 10th Anniversary Edition, xvii.

7   St. Angela Merici, as quoted at http://www.nhregister.com/opinion/20140110/a-new-you-god-is-stretching-out-his-saving-hand-to-you, accessed September 4, 2015.

8   St. Jean Vianney, as quoted at http://www.catholictradition.org/Saints/saintly-quotes21.htm, accessed September 4, 2015.

9   Bernard of Clairvaux, *The Letters* (London: Burns & Oates, 1958), 156.

10   St. Paul of the Cross, *Letters of St. Paul of the Cross,* L. I, 418 in the *Letters of St. Paul of the Cross, Volume 1, 1720-1747* (PassionateProvincial Office, 2000) as quoted at https://passionistcharism.wordpress.com/2009/12/13/, accessed September 4, 2015.

11   An excellent resource for this chapter was Elizabeth Liebert, *The Way of Discernment: Spiritual Practices for Decision Making* (Westminster: John Knox Press, 2008).

12   Frederick Buechner, *Now and Then* (San Francisco: HarperCollins, 1991), 87.

13   Bernard of Clairvaux, *St. Bernard on the Song of Songs: Sermones in Cantica Canticorum,* A. R. Mowbray, trans. (New York: Morehouse-Gorham, 1952), 162.

14   Henri Nouwen, *Reaching Out: The Three Movements of the Spiritual Life* (New York: Doubleday, 1986), 137.

15   Thomas Merton, "My Argument with the Gestapo," as quoted in *Scribbles on the Wall: Lessons Along the Way, A Collaboration of Thoughts by Evan Sutter* (Melbourne, Oceania: Tenth Street Press Ltd., 2013), 99.

16   Joseph Ratzinger, "Abscheid vom Teufel?" in *Dogma und Verkundigung* (Munich: Wewel, 1973), 225–34.

17   Pope Francis, Homily, Rizal Park, Manila, Philippines, Sunday, January 18, 2015.

18   St. John of the Cross, *The Collected Works of St. John of the Cross,* Kieran Kavanaugh, OCD, and Otilio Rodriguez, OCD, trans. (Washington, DC: Institute of Carmelite Studies, 1991), "The Sayings of Light and Love," no. 102, p. 92.

19   Pope Francis, Christmas Address to the Roman Curia, December 22, 2014.

20 Kathleen Norris, *Acedia and Me: A Marriage, Monks, and a Writer's Life* (New York: Riverhead Books, 2008), 42.

21 Archbishop Fulton Sheen, as quoted at http://www.catholicbible101.com/archbishopsheenquotes.htm, accessed September 4, 2015.

22 François Fénelon, *The Complete Fénelon* (Paraclete Giants), Robert J. Edmonson and Hal M. Helms, trans. (Brewster, MA: Paraclete Press, 2008), 16.

23 C. S. Lewis, *The Problem of Pain* (New York: HarperCollins, 2001), 91.

24 Mother Teresa of Calcutta, as quoted in Sheila Walsh, *God Loves Broken People: (And Those Who Pretend They're Not)* (Nashville: Thomas Nelson, 2012), 80.

25 Basil of Caesarea, as quoted in James Lawrence, STB, *Prayers for Help: A Sacred Heart Prayer Book* (Kindle Edition, Lulu.com, September 6, 2014), page unnumbered.

26 Attributed to Augustine of Hippo, as quoted at http://www1.villanova.edu/villanova/mission/campusministry/spirituality/resources/spirituality/restlesshearts/prayers.html, accessed September 4, 2015.

27 Anselm of Canterbury, adapted from *Proslogion*, 1, as quoted at http://www.vatican.va/spirit/documents/spirit_20000630_anselmo_en.html, accessed September 4, 2015.

28 Francis of Assisi, as quoted at http://www.liturgies.net/saints/francis/writings.htm#Oratio, accessed September 4, 2015.

29 Attributed to Ignatius of Loyola, as quoted at http://www.thinkingfaith.org/articles/20120217_1.htm, accessed September 4, 2015.

30 Teresa of Avila, as quoted in Lucinda Vardey, *The Flowering of the Soul: A Book of Prayers by Women* (Toronto, ON: Alfred A Knopf Canada, 1999), 286.

31 John Henry Newman, adapted by the author from a citation from *Meditations and Devotions*, "Meditations on Christian Doctrine," "Hope

in God—Creator," March 7, 1848, as quoted at http://www.newmanreader
.org/works/meditations/meditations9.html#note1, accessed September 4,
2015.

32   Charles de Foucauld, as quoted in Cathy Wright, LSJ, *Charles de Foucauld:
Journey of the Spirit* (Boston: Pauline Books & Media, 2005), 78.

33   Thérèse of Lisieux, as quoted in Woodeene Koenig-Bricker, *Praying with
the Saints: Making Their Prayers Your Own* (Chicago: Loyola Press, 2001),
221.

34   Thomas Merton, *Thoughts in Solitude*, as quoted in Basil Pennington,
editor, *Thomas Merton: I Have Seen What I Was Looking For: Selected
Spiritual Writings* (Hyde Park, NY: New City Press, 2005), 57–58.

35   Mother Teresa of Calcutta, *A Simple Path*, compiled by Lucinda Vardey
(New York: Ballantine Books, 1995), 82.

ABOUT PARACLETE PRESS

Paraclete Press is a publisher of books, recordings, and DVDs on Christian spirituality. Our publishing represents a full expression of Christian belief and practice—from Catholic to Evangelical, from Protestant to Orthodox.

We are the publishing arm of the Community of Jesus, an ecumenical monastic community in the Benedictine tradition. As such, we are uniquely positioned in the marketplace without connection to a large corporation and with informal relationships to many branches and denominations of faith.

WHAT WE ARE DOING

Paraclete Press Books | Paraclete publishes books that show the richness and depth of what it means to be Christian. Although Benedictine spirituality is at the heart of all that we do, we publish books that reflect the Christian experience across many cultures, time periods, and houses of worship. We publish books that nourish the vibrant life of the church and its people.

We have several different series, including the best-selling Paraclete Essentials and Paraclete Giants series of classic texts in contemporary English; Voices from the Monastery—men and women monastics writing about living a spiritual life today; award-winning poetry; best-selling gift books for children on the occasions of baptism and first communion; and the Active Prayer Series that brings creativity and liveliness to any life of prayer.

Mount Tabor Books | Paraclete's newest series, Mount Tabor Books, focuses on liturgical worship, art and art history, ecumenism, and the first millennium church, and was created in conjunction with the Mount Tabor Ecumenical Centre for Art and Spirituality in Barga, Italy.

Paraclete Recordings | From Gregorian chant to contemporary American choral works, our recordings celebrate the best of sacred choral music composed through the centuries that create a space for heaven and earth to intersect. Paraclete Recordings is the record label representing the internationally acclaimed choir Gloriæ Dei Cantores, praised for their "rapt and fathomless spiritual intensity" by *American Record Guide*; the Gloriæ

Dei Cantores Schola, specializing in the study and performance of Gregorian chant; and the other instrumental artists of the Gloriæ Dei Artes Foundation.

Paraclete Press is also privileged to be the exclusive North American distributor of the recordings of the Monastic Choir of St. Peter's Abbey in Solesmes, France, long considered to be a leading authority on Gregorian chant.

Paraclete Video | Our DVDs offer spiritual help, healing, and biblical guidance for a broad range of life issues including grief and loss, marriage, forgiveness, facing death, bullying, addictions, Alzheimer's, and spiritual formation.

Learn more about us at our website:
www.paracletepress.com,
or call us toll-free at 1-800-451-5006.

SCAN TO READ MORE

Come, Follow Me DVD
Six Responses to the Call of Jesus

ISBN: 978-1-61261-654-4 | $89.95 | 180-minute DVD

Albert Haase, OFM, highlights six of the most vital spiritual traditions in the history of the Church: Benedictines, Cistercians, Carmelites, Dominicans, Franciscans, and Jesuits.

Saying Yes DVD
Discovering and Responding to God's Will in Your Life

ISBN: 978-1-61261-760-2 | $89.95 | 180-minute DVD

Albert Haase, OFM, offers six 30-minute segments on the ongoing process of discovering and responding to God's will in your life.

Catching Fire, Becoming Flame DVD

A Guide for Spiritual Transformation

ISBN: 978-1-61261-295-9 | $89.95 | 180-minute DVD

This DVD contains six 30-minute segments:
1. Spiritual Journey as a Process of Transformation
2. Your Image of God
3. The Examen
4. The 7 Principles of Prayer
5. The Challenge of Forgiveness
6. God's Will

Keeping the Fire Alive DVD

Navigating Challenges in the Spiritual Life

ISBN: 978-1-61261-566-0 | $89.95 | 180-minute DVD

This DVD contains six 30-minute segments:
1. Near Occasions of Grace and Spiritual Direction
2. Resisting Temptations
3. Dryness, Darkness, Desolation, or Depression
4. Making Sense of Suffering
5. Living in the Present Moment
6. The Agenda of the Ego